Dancing On The Shore

Dancing
On The Shore

A Celebration of Life at Annapolis Basin

Harold Horwood
With a Foreword by Farley Mowat

M&S   A DOUGLAS GIBSON BOOK

This book is for my youngest child
Leah
whose strange fate it is to have an
Ancient Prophet for a father.

Canadian Cataloguing in Publication Data
Horwood, Harold, 1923–
    Dancing on the shore

ISBN 0-7710-4202-7

1. Natural history – Nova Scotia – Annapolis Basin.
2. Philosophy of nature. I. Title.

QH106.2.N62H67 1987   574.9716'33   C87-093956-4

Printed and bound in Canada by John Deyell Co.

A Douglas Gibson Book
McClelland and Stewart
The Canadian Publishers
481 University Avenue
Toronto M5G 2E9

Contents

Foreword

by Farley Mowat

I deplore the condescending, often-contemptuous use of the term 'nature writer' when it is applied, as it generally is, in an attempt to categorize and stigmatize writers whose interests embrace all of life instead of being limited to the human navel-gazing ordained for us by the guardians of Literary Holy Writ.

Having established this caveat, I am overjoyed to have the opportunity to introduce a man who is incontestably one of the best 'nature writers' of our times.

Harold Horwood has the enormous good fortune to be a Newfoundlander, born and bred. This means that he grew up in a time and place where he and his kind had not made much 'progress' in disassociating themselves from the common matrix of animate creation. Until they were dragged into modernity as a result of the Island's confederation with Canada in 1949, outport Newfoundlanders still retained the psychic, spiritual, and physical connection to the living world of which mankind is but a part. They had not succumbed to the insane belief that we human beings are a special creation set apart over and above, and intrinsically different from, the beasts of the land, birds of the air, fishes of the sea. The outport Newfoundlander, always in intimate contact with other living beings, knew them for what they were – kith and kin. This was not conscious knowledge. It was felt knowledge; an unspoken, inner comprehension which enabled the fisherman working his hand line from a tiny dory adrift in the grey immensity of the North Atlantic to know and to draw strength from the knowledge that he belonged to a living world around, under, and above him. Belonged. It is a key word in the lexicon and in the natural philosophy of people who have not yet cast themselves out from the community of life. A Newfoundlander does not ask (or did not ask) where you come from – he asks where and to what do you belong.

Harold Horwood knows where he belongs. He is a consciously and indissolubly integral part of the vast assemblage of living beings who populate this planet. He is one with all of life and, being so, will never find himself alone in the ever-narrowing confines which technological man has chosen to inhabit. He rests secure that he is not, and never can be, alone. But he is not smug in his assurance, nor does he wear his own kind of blinkers. He is a modern man in the sense that he has a brilliant and inquiring intellect, leavened with compassion, which ranges over the entire living spectrum, and which he has concentrated as much upon his own species as upon those others who so vastly surpass us in kind and numbers.

Horwood writes – has written, and I pray will long continue to write – about all of us, finned, feathered, furred, and naked, with a unique combination of intellect and empathy, building bridges over the steadily widening chasm which separates most of us from awareness of who and what we truly are. He writes lucid, beautiful, celebratory prose, which is nevertheless imbued with an apostolic fervour – for he understands that if we do not bridge the growing gulf, we will become aliens on this planet, and there will be small hope for us.

I have been an admirer of Horwood for thirty years, but never has my admiration for the man and his works burned brighter than it does now, after reading Dancing On The Shore. I believe that with this book he has built a bridge that will endure. I invite you to cross it.

F.M.
April 1987

Author's
Preface

In this century, amidst some of the worst atrocities of human history, we have developed a sense of conscience toward the world and its non-human inhabitants. Somehow, we have achieved the sensibility to condemn and eventually outlaw such monstrous activities as harpooning whales and skinning newborn seals under their mothers' noses. It could not have happened in the nineteenth century, or even in the earlier part of the twentieth. The sense that we are fellow-travellers with the rest of the living world is something entirely new. A hundred years ago a few people understood this in their heads; only now have millions of people begun to feel it in their guts.

When I wrote The Foxes of Beachy Cove *twenty years ago, the liberation of the intellect had not yet happened. The right to publish the products of fundamental creative thinking was limited, in those days, to the small crew who had been given a licence to think: professional scientists and philosophers. The rest of us were supposed merely to interview or quote them. In that book I sang small, limiting myself to what a 'nature writer' might be permitted to say. So although this book is in a sense a sequel to the earlier one, it is also basically different. This is a 'new age' book in which the author drops the mask of journalistic modesty and admits without a blush that he is dealing in new ideas and in the wisdom that comes from a lifetime of reading and discussing the products of human thought from Lao-Tzu of the sixth century B.C. to Ken Wilber, the contemporary philosopher of physics. In these pages you must bear with me not only when I discuss the probable reasons for the brilliant colours of* a finch, but when I discuss the nature of life, and reasons for believing that popular science interpreters have grossly misled their public about the history and development of the genus Homo. I hope that here and there I have provided flashes of insight that will help to illuminate the surrounding darkness.

During the first half of this century the illuminati were banished to obscure corners of universities or to even more obscure niches in religious cults. We have to thank the rebellious children of the sixties (as we have to thank them for so much else) that they brought the prophets back into the human mainstream. Not all their prophets were very good ones, and not all the utterances of even the best of them is Truth, but at least they are thought-provoking, and they point us toward deeper understanding of ourselves, including our extensions outward through space and backward and forward through time. This book is about those extensions, as well as about the joys of living in one of the truly lovely places of the earth.

My decision to publish a second book of wisdom, after twenty years and a dozen lesser books, did not come easily. Like many other people who can write fiction, I had absorbed an exaggerated view of the importance of the novel. I wrote three novels and a book of short stories before I realized that I would rather have written Walden than all the novels published in English in the nineteenth century. This realization made me wonder why I was dabbling in magic realism and visionary fiction when obviously what I wanted to do was present ideas stark naked, not dressed for a masquerade ball. So I went back to my notebooks and looked on beauty bare, and found that a naturalist's observations and ideas, presented in imaginative prose, could thrill and delight me in a way that my most-anthologized short story never could do.

It was with great diffidence that I went before an audience to read, for the first time, a chapter from the manuscript that would later become this book, and found that I was not alone. People in the audience wept. Others came forward to embrace me. I am indebted to the people of Annapolis Royal, Wolfville, and Halifax for convincing me that it was worth pursuing a distant and difficult goal. So here I am, with all my defences down – well, nearly all – offering such bread and wine as I possess to those who are ready to partake of the communion of all life.

A renewal of faith – a restatement of the covenant that binds man to moth and star – a renewed basis for the certainty that we are not in a random and irrational universe – a cure, in fact, for the city sickness that afflicts so much of humanity, *those vast numbers of our species who are cut off from the world, living in the iron lungs and kidney machines and oxygen tents of technological society without connection either to heaven or to earth: that is the aim of this book.*

During the Second World War there was a phenomenon called the 'failure of nerve' of the intellectuals. One of its symptoms was a retreat into the beliefs and rituals of an older orthodoxy. Something similar happened in the 1980s: not a failure of nerve, but an abdication of intellectual responsibility. It became fashionable to view life as though it might be a decadent contemporary novel, a pastiche of random happenings with no plot line and no standards against which to judge its success or failure – a view that is not merely a fad among the au courant set, but a stance actually accepted by some scientists and philosophers and many critics as the basis for their thought. If those with intellectual reputations, who ought to be leaders, can offer nothing better than such nihilism, it is no wonder that millions of uneducated people have fled back to the religious quacks for some kind of reassurance that their lives are not utterly worthless and meaningless.

The come-to-Jesus freaks of the TV circuit, the om-sayers, the flying-saucer cultists, have all benefited by the failure, the refusal, of the intellectuals to offer leadership. The smart journalists who wring their hands over the election of born-again fundamentalists to the White House are the same people who publish, or who encourage the publication of, columns of nihilistic criticism, and present it as the cream of contemporary thought.

Why has it happened? Perhaps it is partly sheer intellectual laziness. It takes a lot of effort to arrive at any positive view of life, at even a very partial understanding of a universe as complex, as truly strange, as ours, but it takes very little effort to look at someone else's interpretation of quantum theory, and to say that since no one can predict when, if ever, an atom of uranium will decay into an atom of lead, therefore events in the universe are random, and no one is responsible for his own life.

But there has been a return to genuine religious content in the thought and the writings of those who have kept faith with their own tradition. Among intellectuals, religious terminology is no longer taboo: when exploring cosmology we can now discuss 'the moment of creation,' and speculate on whether 'god throws dice' or creates freedom. In high intellectual circles you are no longer branded a religious nut when you express humility before the Mystery, or amazement at the arrogance of nineteenth-century scientists who thought they had solved the universe. The great physicists of this century – Planck, Pauli, Einstein, Bohr, Schrödinger – were all men with a deeply religious cast of mind. Their convictions have finally filtered down to the science interpreters, and have doubtless influenced such contemporary thinkers as Fritjof Capra, giving them a profound respect for the pre-Christian philosophers who shaped Hindu and Buddhist thought and wrote the TDao-teh-King. We have begun to believe that all roads, if you pursue them far enough, lead to god.

I am not returning in this book to the pre-Christian philosophers or the medieval mystics (much as I respect both), but I am looking at the world of the Annapolis Basin and its universal connections from my own point of view, reached after twenty-four years of constant meditation in the midst of the real world, and daily association with diverse representatives of the animal and vegetable kingdoms of our living planet. I have not achieved serenity, but I have achieved conviction, a faith as unshakable as that of any apostle or prophet, and a desire to share the vision with those who may wish to see.

Like any other talent, a talent for the direct apprehension of the universe may remain hidden, undeveloped, undiscovered, until a chance event reveals it, or until some master says to the disciple, 'Behold the grass!' This is what Hindus call 'the opening of the spiritual eye,' an event that sometimes follows long training in the spiritual arts. It is sometimes achieved without effort, but always alters profoundly the consciousness of the person concerned, creating what those who experience it regard as life's greatest enrichment.

It used to be fashionable for scientists and their followers, adhering to a simplistic model of the universe as a mere mechanism, to dismiss all this as self-delusion. The fashion is changing. It's as absurd for the spiritually blind to pass such judgments on spiritual matters as it is for the tone-deaf to condemn music as noise. Today many of those fully at home with quantum theory and general relativity have experienced the opening of the spiritual eye. It's heart, not mind, that must be humble and child-like, and there has been a great revival of humility, of awe and wonder, among the world's thinkers.

Freud dismissed all religious feeling as an atavistic relic of childhood. Jesus said it without Freud's semantics: 'Except ye become as little children ye cannot enter the kingdom of heaven.' But what is the kingdom of heaven? The Zen Buddhist might call it satori. I would tend to call it a sense of the expanded self, a sense of the self expanded into the universe, the experience of the cricket and the mouse and Capella and Arcturus and the Ursa Major galaxies as extensions of your fingers and toes. Little children often have a sense of participation in that part of the self that adults have learned to treat as 'the other.' Without recapturing that sense, the spiritual eye is never opened, and the self remains a small capsule in an alien universe, cut off, rejected, 'damned.' If the capsule can be dissolved, the person may see, for the first time, through the eyes of the cricket, and so enter the kingdom of heaven.

People see the world in radically different ways, and many seemingly contradictory visions are more or less valid. I think of the world as seen by Thoreau, a world of almost impeccable order and perfection, marred only by human foolishness; the world as seen by Darwin, an everlasting struggle in which every creature from plant to man is engaged in lethal battle for the right to live and reproduce; the world as seen by Henry Miller, full of magic and mystery and the wonders of the irrational; the world as seen by Sacheverell Sitwell, a nightmare, all bits and pieces of darkness and torture, a bleeding hand, a severed foot, an empty eye-socket spilling pus into a trash can. Four more radically separate, more mutually exclusive views of the world could hardly be imagined, and yet, all four of them have major elements of truth. Truth is never whole, never complete, always like a line drawing without shading, or an abstract-impressionist painting from the 1950s, a fusion of colours without form.

The universe is far too complex to be comprehended in a work like The Origin of Species, or a meditation like Walden, or a Nexus trilogy, or a Journey to the Ends of Time. All any of us can do is project the abstract image of the world that we find mirrored within ourselves, hoping it will enrich others whose images are somewhat like it and at the same time somewhat different. I find it hard to imagine Thoreau even reading The Rosy Crucifixion, or Darwin making any kind of sense out of The Dance of the Quick and the Dead. But there are many of us who can sit, quietly contemplating the world and receiving a gleam here, a spark there, from such diverse sources. With no hobby-horse of our own to ride, we can enjoy a brief canter on each of the many creations offered by the great barkers at the vanity fair.

Before acknowledging some of the gleams and sparks that went into this book, I prefix a word of caution: it doesn't do to treat any writer as a fountain of divine inspiration. Thoreau, for all his clear-headed sanity, occasionally wrote non-sense. Loren Eiseley, for all his penetration, sometimes rode hobbies that will not bear examination, sometimes accepted myths that lead toward darkness rather than light. Every time we read a paragraph that aspires toward truth our critical sense should be awake, for a writer is never more likely to be wrong than when he states what appears to him to be axiomatic. I might mention the 'stern respect' of Thoreau's puritan ethic, Eiseley's Nordic myth of modern man shaped by the ice age, Kirkegaard's doctrine of the redemptive value of suffering, Blake's belief that with the passing of 'empire . . . the lion and the wolf shall cease,' Freud's assumption that the psychic patterns of Victorian Europe could be projected across the whole of humanity and back into prehistory. Such faults are to be found in every writer I admire, from Plotinus to Djuna Barnes. I would have to go back to such legendary sages as Lao-Tzu to find thinkers and writers with whom I agree completely – but then, I suspect that their work has been severely pruned by time. . . .

A book like this, a product of all the reading and thinking its author has ever done, cannot acknowledge most of its sources or the indebtedness of the writer to all those who have shaped his ideas. There are, however, a few specific debts I would like to acknowledge.

The germ of the idea developed in my chapter on the forests, that man is the product of his own vision, occurred to me while I was reading an essay by Loren Eiseley in which he argued against the view that human nature is determined by the human heritage, and proposed that it is more likely to be determined by human wishes or desires.

My model for the nature of matter goes back to the early 1940s, when I discussed this question with my brother, Charles Horwood, a theoretical thinker, and reached what then seemed to be the absurd conclusion that fundamental particles are centres of potential standing waves: places where they would exist 'if there were any medium for them.' This idea was strengthened when I read Pierre Teilhard de Chardin, who expressed the view: 'every particle fills any space we may imagine it to be in,' leading to my own final expression: 'every particle is the centre of an infinite field.' From this concept a holistic universe follows.

I am indebted to the physicist Fritjof Capra for his parallel between the dance of Shiva and the continuous creation and destruction of subatomic particles. Without Capra I might never have acknowledged mesons among the species that dance on the shore of Annapolis Basin.

From Charles Fort I took the important concept that all boundaries in nature are human creations, even the boundary between the living and the lifeless, so that an accretion of crystalline gypsum may properly be regarded as 'the first rough sketch of a rose.'

Alan Watts introduced me to Zen Buddhism more than forty years ago, and led me to read Lao-Tzu and Chuang-Tzu, whose writings have influenced me profoundly. Though I came to mystical experience by my own route, and with subsequent guidance from Watts, I encountered the literature of Christian mysticism *for the first time when Aldous Huxley published* The Perennial Philosophy. *Huxley's writing led me to admit that my thinking about science and nature is deeply coloured by the unitive knowledge of god's immanence in the universe.*

The great Canadian ornithologist L. M. Tuck taught me to observe nature at first hand. If I can be said to have received any scientific training, it was while working as his field assistant and editor.

Werner Heisenberg's non-technical writing has been, for me, a source of intellectual nourishment, and especially his lucid descriptions of the thought of such physicists as Planck and Pauli.

I owe a good deal to the pioneering naturalists Nicolas Tinbergen and Konrad Lorenz, and something to such notable dissenters as Sally Carrighar, who spoke out courageously against the mechanistic view of biology while mechanism was still the only acceptable orthodoxy.

Lastly I must acknowledge the lifelong support and encouragement of my friend and companion Farley Mowat, whose great-hearted views on the rights of other species have influenced my own, and whose comments on the early drafts of this book helped to bring it to completion.

H.H.

Annapolis Basin

March 1987

Dancing On The Shore

1

A Thing So Marvellous to See

Annapolis Basin is a tightly enclosed arm of the sea on the south shore of the Bay of Fundy, which runs northeastward from the Gulf of Maine between the Canadian provinces of New Brunswick and Nova Scotia. The basin is a narrow triangle, eight miles wide at the fishing port of Digby, tapering toward Annapolis Royal, fifteen miles away.

Inland from Goat Island the basin is usually called Annapolis River, though in fact it is still part of the sea. It makes more sense to regard the river as starting above Annapolis causeway, though even there the water is still briny and strongly tidal in a section that is called the French Basin from the fact that the Acadians settled and cultivated its shores, and drained and dyked its tidal marshes back in the seventeenth century.

The Acadian dykes, extending down both shores almost to the region of Port Royal, and up-river to Belleisle, are remarkable works containing millions of tons of earth dug by hand and moved into position by hand labour with the help of oxen and horses. These dykes, built to reclaim low-lying land from the sea, are not simple sea walls. From the start they were fitted with huge valves allowing the rivers to drain outward into the basin, while closing automatically against the incoming tides, an engineering device the French settlers had learned in

Europe, farming tidal flats where the sea rose in floods only a little less sweeping than those of Fundy. The peasants who performed this awesome feat, often working knee-deep in water, must have laboured mightily through generations to complete it. Yet, they much preferred this kind of work to the labour of clearing forest land with axe and saw and plough as English settlers did everywhere they went, then and later.

The French peasants who arrived here in 1605 were husbandmen who had raised sheep and cattle on the salt marshes of northwestern France. They also grew some grain, but what they wanted above all in Acadia was pasture. Once the salt marsh was dyked and drained and desalted by rainfall and river flow, it required no further work; it would provide excellent pasture for all time to come.

When the dykes were up and the valves in place, the desalting happened automatically; within two years the salt marsh was a salt-free meadow, growing red clover and purple vetch and timothy in place of the coarse *Spartina* grasses which had been the dominant plants previously. My neighbours who live along the inner shore of the basin are still pasturing herds of animals on the old Acadian meadow land, most of which has never been fertilized in the past three centuries.

It is worth remembering that when those dykes were first built, the plough as we know it had not yet been invented. Except for the ox-cart and the stake harrow, neither had any other piece of agricultural machinery. Wooden ploughs, with no mouldboards, sometimes had iron plates to make them more durable, but even the stake harrows still had wooden teeth. A metal spade was a prized possession. Not until the time of Jethro Tull (the turn of the eighteenth century) did farmers have even simple agricultural machinery. Till then every farm job except ploughing and hauling was done entirely by hand.

So it seems all the more impressive that the Acadian settlers were able not just to wrest a living from their former salt marshes, but to flourish, to become prosperous, to raise large families, to increase from a few hundred immigrants to a population numbering tens of thousands. This is a region where people willing to co-operate with nature can achieve self-sufficiency, even modest affluence.

The salt marshes alone would not have made the Annapolis Basin the best site for a colony in eastern Canada, indeed, the only place where an early colony succeeded without support from Europe. The other element in its success was the enfolding hills. North and south along river and basin the valley is entrenched between steep ridges. Rising to 850 feet, these hills are locally called 'mountains,' though they are really just wooded hogbacks. With none of the character, much less the height, of mountains, they nevertheless serve to create a very favourable local climate. The sea, flowing in through Digby Gap with tides rising more than twenty-five feet and flooding up-river for almost thirty miles, softens the winter and extends the summer. At the same time the enfolding hills protect the region from cold winds, especially from north winds off the Bay of Fundy, whose only access to the valley is by way of the one narrow funnel at Digby.

So the whole region from Digby to Belleisle enjoys a micro-climate rather like that of regions some hundreds of miles to the south, less like that of Maine, let us say, than of coastal Connecticut. It is, consequently, not only a good place for raising animals, but also for gardening. Such vegetables as tomatoes, peppers, and squash flourish mightily on the shores of Annapolis Basin. During the first two weeks of April the woods are scented by the lilac-coloured flowers of a wild shrub, Daphne mezereon, that came from the warm shores of the Mediterranean by way of France or England, and soon made itself at home here. The winters are mild enough for broad-leafed evergreens like hollies to flourish, and the summers cool enough for crops such as pod peas that cannot stand heat. Gardeners on the shores of the basin regularly grow ornamental shrubs not normally seen north of coastal Massachusetts or New Hampshire. Whoever first planted peach trees on these shores must have been amazed at their success. A few of us even grow melons beside our patches of corn, potatoes, and peas.

The combination of sheltering hills, moderating sea water, fertile riverbottom soil, and salt marshes, created the conditions for Canada's first successful agricultural colony, and continues to provide the conditions for home gardening and small farming in this most favoured region. The French pioneers at Port Royal did their experimental gardening somewhere 'up-river' near Lequille, and built their first grist-mill on the Lequille River which enters the basin at Annapolis Royal. Marc Lescarbot, the Paris lawyer who visited the colony during its second year, and later wrote the history of New France, reported success with every kind of crop from Indian corn to marijuana (perhaps grown mainly for fibre).

A region supporting such a lush and varied growth of plants provides equally well for wild animals. White-tailed deer and varying hares are almost pests in this area (some gardeners would omit the 'almost'). My own orchard has been visited, without serious harm, by black bears, bobcats, porcupines, raccoons, otters, and pine martens, among others. The whole basin – indeed the whole Fundy shore – is a gathering and feeding ground for flocks of migrating shorebirds that literally number millions.

Unless you've been born here, you can never get used to the tides. Twice a day they come creeping up to cover rocks that towered far overhead a few hours before, until the basin is filled to the edge of the fields with a great flood. Then it seems to empty itself; the water vanishes over the clam flats; before you know it, what's left truly looks like a river rather than an arm of the sea. Once or twice a month even the last remaining strips of beach will disappear, and once or twice a year the water will inundate the salt marshes and come creeping up into the meadows.

Great schools of fish come surging with the tides through Digby Gap, and in pioneer times were perhaps just as important as the resources of the land. A few fish traps still stand around the basin: towering nets strung on poles, often shaped like corrals, to trap the fish, then net them by the gills. In early times such traps lined the shores from Annapolis Royal to Digby, but today most fishing is done from trawlers and longliners out in the bay.

To one accustomed to the awesome seascapes visible from the hills above Beachy Cove in Newfoundland, and to the scarred face of Beachy Cove Mountain, its great slabs of rock dyed red by the setting sun, the Annapolis Basin seems tame and almost pastoral. Yet it is in its own way exceptional. The Goat Island 'runs,' the little coves between Ryerson Brook and Porter's Point, the near and distant hills of the far shore, all combine to create a landscape rather like one painted by Constable at his best.

'A thing so marvellous to see, I wonder how so fair a place did remain uninhabited,' Marc Lescarbot said of Annapolis Basin. The French lawyer and historian was thinking of cities and towns; the basin was already inhabited in his time, but to European colonists Indians didn't count as inhabitants. Even the most sympathetic, like Lescarbot, couldn't help thinking of them as part of the wild fauna, like the deer and the geese. The idea that they might *own* the place, and be making full use of it in the best possible way, would never have crossed his mind. Now, gazing across the basin from which the Indians have long departed (and from which the French, in turn, were driven at bayonet-point), I wonder if it did not truly belong to them in a sense that Europeans have never been able to understand – in the same sense that it belonged to the lynx and the wood bison and the white-tailed deer.

Especially in the light of evening, before or after sunset, the basin from our vantage point suggests harmony and peace, symmetry and the repetition of pleasant rhythms. On this shore one is not overawed by the sheer power of nature, as one is awed in coastal Newfoundland or Cape Breton during or after a northeast gale. Here I am impressed less by the power of nature than by its fecundity: aspens that put on seven feet of growth in a single summer, an alder shoot that rises from the ground at the end of April and grows *an inch a day* so that it towers twelve feet high in autumn, a bank of soil left by a bulldozer that clothes itself in a single season in ferns and rushes and the lovely flowers of jewelweed hanging higher than your head. You feel here that nature will not be put down, that the ugliness, the scars, and the devastation are only temporary blemishes that this great tide of life will cover and soften and make beautiful almost in the time it takes the would-be destroyer to turn away and light a cigarette or open a bottle of beer.

The basin is a kind of private world, bounded on the northeast by the villages of Annapolis Royal and Granville Ferry, on the southwest by the town of Digby. North of Annapolis the valley widens out, becomes flat, almost feature-less farmland; south of Digby is the open roadstead of St. Mary's Bay, its arms spread wide to the Atlantic Ocean. The basin, lying between, is a kind of Mediterranean Sea in minia-ture, separated from the ocean by its own Pillars of Hercules. Inside those walls of stone the earth is a world apart, where wildflowers bloom in March and grapes ripen in October.

It is easy to fall in love with this small world, as I discovered one day in January after I had lived here for less than two years, and had been away for almost four months. A friend picked me up at the ferry dock in Digby, and drove me past The Joggins and Bear Island, the reefs of Fool's Run and the channels of the Goat Island Gap, to my home at Upper Clements, and I realized, as we drove, how deeply attached I had become to the whole region. I was not merely coming home, but coming back to a place that spoke to me at the deepest levels, as Beachy Cove had spoken to me before – a place that had a great deal to say about the phenomenal universe and how it fits together, growing in marvellous harmony out of the unitary universe from which it is derived. Here, if I were willing to be still and listen, I might detect voices speaking out of meadow and marsh, forest and sea, and out of the star-lit darkness.

The colony that built Port Royal on the banks of Goat Island Run in 1605 failed because of attacks by privateers from New England. The Habitation was abandoned. But only briefly. Fur traders and other adventurers, and peaceful settlers, found the area so attractive, and the Micmac Indians so foolishly co-operative, that they soon established themselves here with little help from the European colonizing companies, which had such a great struggle planting their trading posts in Newfoundland (where they had begun trying it more than a hundred years earlier, and still weren't succeeding), and in Quebec and in what are now the American states. The struggle to survive here was not a question of combating a hostile environment or fighting off the natives; it was a question of fighting off pirates, privateers, and the agents of rival fur companies. The rebuilt Habitation at Port Royal, the restored Fort Anne at Annapolis, and the restored grist-mill on the Lequille River (now grinding out electricity instead of meal) are all attractive mementoes of early colonization, demonstrating its solid and purposeful nature. Europeans came to this place not as mere traders and transients, but with the firm intention of making it their permanent home.

In recent years Annapolis Royal has indulged in a positive orgy of restoration, repairing and redecorating its Victorian and Edwardian buildings in something like their original splendour, even creating new 'restorations' such as the Historic Gardens, which have scant basis in history, but are masterpieces of landscaping anyway.

The Habitation at Port Royal is a beautiful restoration: hand-hewn beams and planks fastened with wooden pegs, hand-hewn wooden furniture, all as it would have been made in the early seventeenth century. Except for the lightning rods on the roof, authenticity could hardly have been carried further.

Nobody seems to have thought of restoring the Micmac village of the chief Membertou, without whom the French colony at Port Royal could not have survived its first winter. The Micmacs, who were the colonists' guides, hunters, and canoemen, accepted a kind of patronizing friendship from the French, but were later killed and driven off by the English. In Nova Scotia, as in all parts of North America colonized by European settlers, the Indians have had a pretty thin time, and have received scant recognition for the great contribution that they made to the nation's development.

As the French power waned, Scots, Irish, and especially New Englanders came flooding into southern Nova Scotia; finally there was an influx of British Empire Loyalists (many of them in no sense British, but all of them hostile to the American Revolution), giving the population its character: settled, conservative, rural, somewhat puritanical, somewhat old-fashioned. Just recently this deep-rooted population has been spiced by an influx of Canadians and Americans belonging to the artistic subculture: painters, musicians, writers, people practising gardening, handicrafts, alternative lifestyles, and generally belonging to the so-called Aquarian Conspiracy. They have settled among people whose ancestors were born here with less friction than you might expect, perhaps because there is in this region a long tradition of courtesy and tolerance, a tradition that you see at work every day on the streets of Annapolis Royal, where motorists automatically stop for any pedestrian who looks as if he wants to cross the street, even in the middle of a block.

Life around the basin is in many ways like it was generations ago, and in many ways different. Rural people today take for granted such things as rapid transit, communications, and travel. Halifax is a place you go to shop, perhaps once a month, instead of a place you visit once or twice in a lifetime, if ever. Farmers and innkeepers go to Florida for the winter. Some children ride trail bikes (and some of them get killed doing it). They have 'fitness' tests in the schools, and for trail-bike riders such tests may even make sense. Here and there a modest-looking house has the interim technology of a parabolic satellite receiver planted in its yard, but to the chagrin of the manufacturers such 'dishes' have not blossomed across the landscape the way TV masts did in the 1950s. People have become justifiably sceptical that the latest technological marvels will remain useful for long, or that they add anything to human happiness in the meantime.

The children who live with us here, and the children who come to visit, do not ride trail bikes. They go running barefoot through the fields and woods. They climb trees. They explore the beaches and splash in the sea. They paddle boats and canoes. They bring into the house such miraculous creatures as rock crabs and red-backed salamanders. All of this was done by Acadian children more than three centuries ago, and by Indian children centuries before that, and is as filled with magic today as it ever was. Such children need neither trail bikes nor fitness tests; they are living in the world, not in a technological fantasy.

Most people inhabit the shores of this basin not from any sense of necessity but because they wish to live here. That makes a big difference to the character of the people. I met a boy recently in the Fort Anne park. He was maybe fifteen or sixteen years old, with long hair, immature beard, bare feet, the sort of kid who would have been persecuted as a 'freak' a generation ago. He talked to me about Annapolis Royal, how much he liked the village, how he hoped he'd be able to stay, though there was every likelihood he'd have to go away to work. I asked him where he'd come from, and he told me he was born here. He added that he never wanted to live anywhere else. How different from those terrible places one reads about, those rural swamps where every boy and girl dreads above all else the danger of being trapped there, where everyone's youthful ambition is to escape to the bright lights of the nearest city!

There is a sense of contentment here, a sense of being in a place where one wants to be, a sense of mild but pervading satisfaction in the generosity of the earth – and among some of us a wish that we could be left alone here, that we could be assured of another human generation to enjoy the plenitude of the land, without the threats of geopolitics and the loom of global disaster.

But perhaps that is the way it has always been in the good places of the earth. The peasant in the Dordogne Valley, the Hunza in his mountain ravine, have always lived with the threat of destruction from the outside.

In 1979 Corky and I and our two young children, Andrew and Leah, decided to settle here. We had visited every province and state in North America. We had lived in several of them. We built our house on the shore of Fool's Run, overlooking Goat Island and the Habitation, because this, of all the places we had been, was the one we preferred. Fool's Run? Well, you see, there are two passages past Goat Island to Annapolis Royal. Ship's Run, taken by all knowledgeable captains, is on the far side. Fool's Run, strewn with reefs and sandbars, is for seals and loons and people like us, who prefer to travel in canoes.

Acadia is the loveliest place in Canada east of the Rockies. I look across the valley in the rain, seeing the ridges rise, the trees green in the foreground, turning pearly gray the higher and more distant they rise. It looks English. A British landscape painter in watercolours would have fun with it: the perspective from a rooftop, three red and white cows for scale and contrast like toys on a child's model of a farm – no human figures in this one; the half-naked peasants, getting ready for their midday frolic in the shadows of the hedge, come out only in the sun; the rain creates pre-Adamic landscapes, echoes of an earth cleaner than this, less cluttered, when the pace of life was measured by moonrise and tidefall, and the sky was not yet welted with the white stripes of commerce, or the blasts of exploding space shuttles.

Here in mid-July, when the air is scented with wild roses, and meadowsweet blooms in the ditches, when the light falls dim and cool through two months' growth of young vines, you could well believe that man and the world grew up together, perfectly suited and matched, until you remember the hellholes of the cities, full of poison and corruption and every known kind of misery. Then you remember that humans not only are 'the growing tip of evolution,' as Pierre Teilhard de Chardin called them, but are also filthy beasts, vicious, late-comers to the earth, perhaps the greatest curse that has ever fallen upon the planet. I will likely die without knowing the resolution of this matter. I will only know it for sure if I die in the nuclear holocaust that so many of our kind are prepared to inflict on the biosphere.

2

Water of Life

For most of its length – at least for that part of it that you can navigate in a boat – the Annapolis River is slow and tidal, snaking its way between banks of mud and grass through a long succession of farms that have been tilled for three and a half centuries. The streams that feed the river have quite a different character. Roaring cascades, they come down the slopes of South Mountain, tumbling over granite boulders, pausing in ponds and lakes whose currents swirl like the winds of cyclones, rushing through cool stands of spruce and pine and hemlock, shouting as they go – until they collapse suddenly into the flat valley, directly from mountain to riverbottom, where they wind sedately through muddy creek beds, being tamed and controlled by the tides until they join the Annapolis River itself, sedate and middle-aged, all shouting and laughter left behind.

Those streams are my kind of river, useless for trade but leaping with trout and dragonfly and kingfisher, home to the eagle and the goshawk, land of the marten and the mink. Along their banks Nova Scotia becomes for a little while like Labrador or the Upper Churchill, wilderness in the original sense, its waters as clear as moonlight, its air scented with the myrrh of evergreens and aloud only with birdsong. It amazes me that men can look at such country and think of it only in terms of what it can contribute to the stinking life of the cities: power for generators, wood for pulp grinders, and pelts for silly women who would be infinitely better off digging in potato fields.

These little rivers are the universe at work. They are the sun making the earth fruitful. They dance because the atoms dance in the vast corona of our star. Their voice is truly the music of the spheres, the joyous song of the solar system brought down to the here and now, singing life, singing its upwelling, proclaiming the great fountain from which they spring, flowing forever out of the heart of darkness with the primal shout: Let there be light!

They are one of the many incarnations of water in our lives, of rivers, of ponds, of ocean, all of them meeting here. Our house stands on a knoll above the sea, flanked on one side by a small marsh filled with wild cranberries and heaven-scented orchids, and on two sides by a wooded ravine containing a small stream, a large collection of bog plants, and two ponds. The entire ravine was once a curving lake that gradually filled with vegetation. This process was greatly accelerated by the building of the railway in the nineteenth century, an engineering feat that cut off much of the water supply. When we arrived our first job was to restore at least a part of the former water flow, and to reclaim sections of the former lake, to create our two ponds.

The ponds brought with them many new species of plants and animals that have added to our delight in living here: to mention just a few, we now have lovely clumps of blue-flag iris, a patch of vivid pickerelweed with arrow-like leaves and spires of blue flowers, patches of white pond lilies that open every morning as the sun touches the water, and clumps of delicate lady's-smock cress. And jewelweed growing wild on the banks has brought hummingbirds to our front door.

The water in the new ponds has attracted mobs of green frogs and spring peepers. The chorus of peepers is one of the great joys of early spring; we sit on our deck in the twilight, listening, proud of the fact that we brought hundreds of these little creatures to our doorstep merely by providing a place for them to live.

The green frogs sit on the banks, sunning themselves, and will allow us to crouch there and watch them, if we do not go too close. They also sit on lily pads, at least while they are still small enough for the pads to support their weight. Later they grow so big and fat that the pads would sink beneath them; then they crouch among the pickerelweed in the shallows. At least one garter snake moves cautiously through the great clumps of ferns that grow on the shady side of the lily pond, probably hunting frogs, or the toads that often resort there in spring. A great blue heron also visits the ponds in summer, waiting with consummate patience for a tadpole. Attracting this magnificent bird to our front garden is one of our great triumphs. If the Prime Minister came visiting we'd be flattered, but not more flattered than we are by the visits of the great blue heron.

The ponds are a source of delight at all seasons. In winter the children skate on the larger and shallower of the two. On the rare occasions when it freezes with a glass-clear surface where you can walk safely (and before that surface is marred by skates) it is a special pleasure to stare down through the 'glass' at the busy creatures pursuing their own affairs below. Tadpoles scuttle from one hiding place to the next, reacting to our presence as they would to the presence of a heron. The children increase the shelter for tadpoles by putting pumpkin shells into the pond before freeze-up, and are amused to see whole schools of tadpoles not only sheltering inside, but gradually eating themselves out of house and home. Water boatmen paddle along under the ice with their strange little oars. Black water bugs hunt along the bottom of the pond. And green plants thrive under the ice, thrusting upwards from the underlying mud like the numberless spires of a miniature forest. Life slows in winter, but does not come to a stop. Down in the mud the adult frogs are deep in hibernation, their breathing halted, absorbing through their skin the minute quantity of oxygen that they need to survive until spring. The engines of their lives are almost stalled, slowed down to a pace we can barely imagine, like the metabolic pace of a dormant plant, but not quite stopped altogether. Down in the mud, too, are the sleeping bugs, some of them adults, many of them larvae, most of them mere eggs, all awaiting the touch of the returning sun, the warm steps of April, to welcome them back to the world of the living from the death-like trance of their winter sleep.

Just once, walking on the frozen surface, I saw an amazing sight – clear lenses in the ice shaped and veined like lily pads – the ghosts of the lilies that had bloomed the summer before. Yellowed and sunken, they had reflected the sunlight and dispersed the fine bubbles in the ice, creating small, perfectly patterned windows through which I could view the bottom.

During the rains of spring the water gurgles down the banks between the clumps of Christmas fern, forming musical waterfalls as it hurries into the lily pond where the first red sprouts are beginning to rise from roots buried far below the surface. It tumbles over the spillway into the ravine, bringing a freight of dissolved air and a little fresh silt to the blue flags and the forget-me-nots and the lady's-smock cress. It babbles down the channels to the second pond, and goes roaring over the lower spillway past the marsh marigolds and the trilliums before tunnelling under a mass of moss-covered rocks and escaping through the woodland to the sea.

Why is running water such balm to the human spirit? Why do we sleep more soundly beside a waterfall than in the quiet forest? Better even than the rainbow, I think, it represents for us the continuing process of life on our planet. The flow of water is the cycle of fertility renewing itself; it happens only because the sun has been shining, the mists rising, and the rains falling in the distant hills. A deep human instinct of involvement in the onward flow of life, of the cyclical movements of nature, has given us this archetype of flowing water, the sound of it telling us that the world is alive, like the sound of a heart beating beside us in sleep.

Still water has its own kind of appeal to the human soul. It represents for us calmness, wisdom, depths, and quietude. The psychoanalysts would try to make it mean something else, but let us ignore them. Beside the still waters is the place for the sage, the philosopher, the prophet, trying to envision, not by trial and error but by contemplation, the inner nature of things.

Ideally, therefore, one has both, the leaping brook that sings aloud of life, and the quiet pond that fosters the silence of the mind. In Japanese gardens the landscape artists strove for both, no matter how small the scale. If they could not manage a leaping brook and a lily pond, they would lead a trickle of water through a bamboo pipe and let it fall, drop by drop, into a tiny pool in the hollow of a rock.

Magic in water. Yes. I remember a gang of boys in the heart of the city of St. John's, shoes and socks discarded somewhere out of sight, splashing in a huge puddle of rainwater in a parking lot behind a government building. A friend of mine – a senior civil servant – glancing out his window referred to the boys as 'dirty little sweeps.' To me they were like the leaping trout in the brook, a little corrupted, perhaps, by the moth and rust of city life, but still part of that fountain pouring out of the darkness that gives birth to the rivers and spreads the rainbow across the sky.

I remember sparrows, even more delirious than the boys, raising a rainbow of spray from a pond over which I could leap with ease. Though we left the ocean half a billion years ago, we have never ceased to live in water. Not only are we mostly water ourselves, but the very air we breathe would destroy us instantly were it not for the invisible water it contains – water ever present, but made visible only from time to time as rain, as mist, as cloud.

If you look attentively at a fish you can see that the water has shaped it. The fish is not merely *in* the water: the qualities of the water itself have called the fish into being. A bird, in much the same way, is a product of the air. Wings are not miraculous machines designed to defeat the atmosphere; they are its very essence. A feather has been called into being by the currents of air, not by any wisdom on the part of the bird, but merely by its ability to yield, to say 'yes' to the world around it.

The fish in the water, the bird in the air, the deer in the forest, all life, in fact, is an expression, a flowering, of the non-living world, and once we set up a conflict between the living and the non-living we at once lose sight of reality and begin shaping a myth.

Life, though a late efflorescence in the development of the universe, profoundly affects the world as a whole. It is not merely the fragile bloom of the world's late summer after a long winter and spring, but from its very inception it has been altering the chemistry of the world. And though the flowering comes late, the inception came early – organic chemistry was evolving in the gases of the solar system before the world condensed out of its cloud of dust and gas. But once life really began to burgeon, to cover the surface of the earth, it completely altered the upper layers of the earth itself, including the chemistry of its miles-thick layer of atmosphere. The sky is blue, and not yellow, because flowers bloom and trees grow and diatoms spread like a gratuitous grace on the surface of the sea. And these in turn exist only because the air-breathing animals, from insect to whale, from earthworm to elephant, replenish the carbon gas from which the basic structure of all plants is formed. For either plants or animals alone, life would be a one-way street, and would have reached a dead end billions of years ago. But they have found a way to go on forever; they live by taking in each other's washing.

We stand between the bird and the fish, between water and air, depending on both, a product of both, shaped as much by the non-living as by the living world, filled with the breath of life, with the 'water of life' which men in past centuries sought in far places, not knowing that it flowed in every stream and ditch, and dripped from every rock along the shore.

Water is the only substance common to our daily lives in all three states – solid, liquid, and gas. The earth's temperature is just right for water, allowing it to exist in all its forms simultaneously. A little hotter, and we would have nothing but gas or vapour, a little colder, and we would have nothing but ice. On this fortunate water planet, we have all three. The glory of the clouds, the beauty of dawn and sunset, the fascination of the snow, all are unique in this solar system to the one planet where water is both plentiful and able to transform itself with ease from vapour to liquid to crystal, or even directly from one extreme state to the other.

Men must have looked at snow crystals and marvelled at their structure since men began to marvel. It is only because of their size that they are not regarded as one of the great wonders of the world. Were they as big as salad plates, instead of as small as sequins, they would be generally appreciated as among the most intricately beautiful structures that we know.

Except for a few primitive crystals that remain as triangles, all snowflakes are six-sided. Beyond that, they are intricate to a degree past imagining. People who have examined and photographed thousands of them report that no two are exactly alike. And yet all this intricate geometry is quite logical and inevitable, and follows directly from the nature of water itself. The water molecule is a triangle with an oxygen atom at one vertex and a hydrogen atom at each of the other two. The pattern of the snowflake is built upon those triangular molecules, and follows directly from the nature of the bonds that hold them together. Water crystallizes in those fanciful shapes because its molecules lock together in the only logical way they can. Every normal snowflake is a star of David formed from two triangles with numbers of smaller ones affixed in regular patterns. It is tempting to suspect that the original six-pointed star with its interlocking triangles was actually inspired by the famous snows of Lebanon.

There is much in the universe that we do not understand, but there is much that we do, and we must not make mysteries where none exist. The shimmering point in space that we call an electron, the point where infinity meets the infinitesimal and creates a resonance that we can perceive, holds already within it the logic of the snowflake in its geometrical perfection and its infinite variety. If we can properly say that god is immanent in the world, then it is mainly at this point of resonance, the infinitesimal standing wave where infinite fields intersect and lay the basis for the material universe that we see and know, whether in its small aspect through an electron microscope, or in its large dimensions, through a radio telescope that probes outward and backward through billions of light years.

3

The Voices of the Night

We had barely arrived on the shores of Fool's Run – indeed, we were still camping in a shed in April, and trying to get the basement of the house floored over so we could camp *there* – when we began hearing calls from our woods that we had never heard in Newfoundland. Some of the awakening creatures whose voices kept us entertained were not hard to identify. They were frogs, though of species different from those at Beachy Cove: leopard frogs, a bullfrog, spring peepers, the curious clucking of the little wood frog, and the quite wonderful song of the common toad.

But one voice that we thought at first might be the voice of a frog was especially puzzling: a deep, hoarse, buzzing 'bzeep,' repeated over and over, loud and insistent at twilight, and continuing into the night.

My nephew Charlie (who was working on the house) became consumed with insatiable curiosity. Eventually he went haring off through the birch and aspen saplings in pursuit of this elusive sound, and, after chasing it hither and yon for a good half-hour, returned triumphant.

'A bird,' he reported.

'A bird? What kind?'

'Well . . . fairly big . . . almost as big as a pigeon. It flew off very fast.'

'Um . . . that helps . . . can't be many kinds of pigeon-sized birds nesting in wet scrubland in Nova Scotia. . . ."

We got out a field guide, began eliminating the birds whose calls we knew, and soon arrived at the woodcock. True enough, I'd seen it before, but only in midsummer, flushed from light cover in Ontario, at a time when it wouldn't be 'singing.'

Soon we were not only hearing the woodcock's vocal squawks, but, far more gratifying, we were listening to the magic sound that falls from its wings at night. Ever since that first spring I have spent hours and hours in the evening darkness listening to the bubbling, trilling, night song of the woodcocks: a song that is not vocal music at all, for the wonder is that this drab-looking bird does its singing with its feathers. Other birds (including grouse, which 'drum') make loud noises with their feathers; the nighthawk makes a sort of boom, the snipe a high-pitched winnowing or bleating, so wild and eerie it can make you catch your breath in wonder. But none of them makes a sound that could properly be called singing. The sounds made by the woodcock's wings are not any sort of booming or whistling in the air; the woodcock makes the most thrilling music. The air plays over its feathers just as the wind plays over the strings of an aeolian harp. The effect falls somewhere between that of a small trilling pipe and a set of bells.

Once I heard this miraculous song I kept hearing it over and over. I hear it on spring evenings at Annapolis Basin almost as frequently as I heard snipe at Beachy Cove. The woodcock sings over its nesting territory during the mating season in a series of zooming flights, with short rests on the ground between, and may continue until midnight, when, I suppose, it falls asleep, exhausted. I feel quite privileged to be sharing my land with such a tenant.

Though the woodcock seems to be less common here than

the snipe is in Newfoundland, where thousands are killed by hunters every autumn, my son Andrew and I have tracked down the territories of four nesting pairs around the borders of our woods and fields. The birds don't seem to be very choosy about their nest sites. Some we found in young hardwood growth, one was in a wild hedge between fields, one was at the edge of dense mixed woodland. Perhaps the willets and the woodcock, together, fill much the same ecological niche here as the snipe fill in Newfoundland – certainly they nest in similar places. The woodcock is one of our earliest migrants. I have seen it here by March 15.

Besides woodcock, we have other 'game' birds nesting here. None of them is 'game' as far as we are concerned. On a walk through my woodlot I sometimes encounter two or three ruffed grouse, and I sometimes see three or four spruce grouse flying together just above the tops of my shrubs, but the spruce grouse is much less common here than in the dense coniferous forests of the wilder parts of Nova Scotia. They are among the least suspicious of wild birds. If you move slowly you can actually walk to within arm's reach of them. The ruffed grouse, rarely seen in the open, is common enough in the woods all along the shores of the basin. It is famous for the booming noise – 'something between a rattle and a drum' – made by the male in mating season – a noise of great volume which many people have refused to believe the bird can produce by merely fanning the air, which in fact is what it does. Dwelling in thickets and woodlots, the ruffed grouse is far better protected than the pheasant from the gun nuts.

We see pheasants not only in our meadow, or the meadow adjoining, but sometimes right beside our back door, like barnyard chickens, only ever so much handsomer. It's the male pheasant you always seem to see. He is almost as conspicuous as a peacock, with a purplish or green iridescent head, bright red wattles that reach up to surround his eyes, a white collar, wings of russet and brown flecked with white, and body feathers of burnt orange. His tail, a bit longer than the rest of his body, is his most distinctive ornament. Like his relative the domestic rooster, the cock pheasant struts and crows, while his sober-hued mate stays out of sight and broods her eggs. Cock pheasants have been seen brooding eggs, but it is a rare event. They are usually too busy admiring their own beauty to attend to such commonplace pursuits.

In this group of birds – pheasants, peacocks, turkeys, domestic fowl – male vanity seems to have reached its peak. Even a young army lieutenant preening before a mirror in his new uniform hardly seems vainer than a cock pheasant on a rock in the dawn turning his head haughtily from side to side to admire his own fluffed-out feathers.

This subtropical bird, native to southern Asia, has taken to the northland with élan. About thirty years ago a few pheasants escaped from a farm near St. John's, Newfoundland. Contrary to expectations, they not only survived, but flourished in the wild. They seem to flourish everywhere. I have seen pheasants on the north shore of Lake Ontario, in prairie grassland, and on top of Mount Royal in the city of Montreal.

The only pheasant's nest I've examined had fourteen eggs – a bit unusual, I'm told, but they frequently lay sets of a dozen, and two or more hens sometimes share a single nest. While their mates are off strutting about the territory, these grass widows are permitted to take solace in each other's company, and to share the baby-sitting, as the mates of more attentive husbands would never be permitted to do.

The size of their broods helps to explain their success in the face of the most fanatical pursuit by hunters. Annual kills of over *two million* pheasants have been recorded by game authorities in a *single* American state. Less common in Canada, they are nevertheless resident right across the country, and are among the game birds most often seen in southwestern Nova Scotia.

More visible than any of those larger birds are the nighthawks, so named because they fly at dusk, 'hawking' for insects in the air. We see them, as a rule, in August, when the young are all fledged, and they are flying in flocks of hundreds together, fattening themselves for the long flight to their winter homes in South America. We sometimes see nighthawks flying in close-knit flocks almost at grass-top level, darting and weaving as they pursue grasshoppers. Once as my wife and I and our two children sat around a campfire, a flock of night-hawks came visiting, flying in swift passes back and forth, first one side, then the other, at no more than eye level, catching moths attracted by the light of the fire. Perhaps they had learned that light attracts insects, for birds are quite capable of changing their instinctive habits when a new supply of food appears. The most remarkable instance of this adaptability I've seen was a robin catching earthworms at *one o'clock in the morning* under a floodlight on a neighbour's lawn. Robins normally sleep all night. This one had discovered the advantage of hunting with an artificial light, like a poacher fishing from a punt.

So nighthawks will come hunting around campfires just after dark, but they are most interesting when chasing mosquitoes, moths, or other flying insects above the rooftops. They seem especially attracted by a hatch of flying ants. A hundred nighthawks wheeling against the sky at dusk like tiny falcons is an impressive sight. In the white light of the afterglow the large white patches on their wings look like holes or lenses. As they hunt they emit loud buzzing or wheezing calls, obviously intended to invite any strays that happen to be in the vicinity to come and join the feast.

During courtship and nesting the nighthawks also produce flight calls with their feathers, but the sound they make could hardly be called a 'song': it might pass for a part in a hillbilly jug band, for it is quite like the sound you can make by blowing across the neck of a one-gallon moonshine jar. Unlike the other birds, the nighthawk produces his aerial 'booming' not high in the sky but at the bottom of a steep dive almost to ground level, where his mate sits, watching and listening to his display.

It would be an interesting project for someone to investigate whether the sex roles among this class of birds are as rigidly fixed as has been usually assumed. Unfortunately, the sexes look so much alike to a human eye that it is next to impossible to distinguish them in the field. Ornithologists assume that any bird performing territorial flights is a male. Wouldn't it be fun to mark a lot of females with fluorescent dye and watch for one of them doing her thing with the boys? Wouldn't it be shocking to find a male sitting on the ground, watching her perform? Stranger things have happened, and I commend this to students in ornithology looking for a spring project.

A number of our patriarchal assumptions about animals have turned out to be wrong. For example, so-called 'harems' – of seals and deer and antelope – are often loose sexual relationships in which females come and go at will. They may include more than one male. Among caribou the sentries, guides, and herd leaders are usually older females, not stags. Female herring gulls defend their territories, and female ravens are aerial acrobats, like their mates. So in spite of the authorities I'm far from sure that only male nighthawks 'boom.'

These birds nest on open rocky ground, or rock ledges, or gravel roofs, and also on burnt-over forest land where the ground cover has not yet regrown. They seem to shun any kind of overhead protection. And 'nest' is hardly the word, for the nighthawk doesn't even bother to push a few pebbles together to mark the spot where she lays her two eggs; what's more, she keeps moving them a little every day until, by the time they hatch, they may be four or five metres from the place she laid them.

She sits so still on her eggs, and looks so exactly like a mottled rock, that you may stare directly at her for minutes at a time and completely fail to see her unless you happen to see an eye blink. The near-perfect camouflage extends to the eggs and the chicks – and the chicks, as well as brooding adults, trust it implicitly. You may step on a nighthawk chick before it will try to run, and you can walk up slowly to a brooding bird and cautiously lift her off her eggs. But if you dash about quickly she may begin to squawk and flap, as though partly disabled, and so lead you away from eggs or chicks that you probably never would have seen anyway. This habit, common to many ground-nesting birds, is believed to be highly effective in luring foxes and cats away from nests.

Perhaps because they have such a long way to migrate, the nighthawks leave our area long before flying insects begin to be scarce. We rarely see them here after the end of August. One evening there are hundreds; next morning there are none. We will see them no more until May, and then only singly or in pairs. The big wheeling flocks are seen only in late summer.

Like snipe today, nighthawks were formerly hunted, not because they were especially choice morsels for the pot, but because they were difficult targets as they chased insects rapidly in a swooping, zigzag flight. They were considered such a challenge that Dr. E. Sterling, writing in 1885, suggested that god had created them especially to sharpen the skills of youthful gunners: 'Their rapid and irregular flight makes them a difficult mark for the young sportsman to practise on, as he never fails to make a target of them when the opportunity offers. I can now understand the object for which this bird was created.'

In spite of its being such a difficult target, sportsmen would often boast of killing 'several hundred' nighthawks during autumn migrations, when flocks wheeled about in dense groups. For several human generations, killing nighthawks was a popular pastime for thousands of boys and young men throughout the American south, where it was a part of the process of brutalization by which boys were conditioned to accept the barbarian culture of their elders. Were, and still are.

Early in this century when it was first noticed that the numbers of nighthawks were declining, they were given legal protection, but that didn't stop the killing. Only when the sportsmen were hauled into court and prosecuted as poachers did they finally quit.

Having run the gauntlet of hot lead all the way along the

American coastline from Maine to Florida, the nighthawks would cross the Gulf of Mexico, the swamps and rivers of South America, and even the great snowy crests of the Andes, to winter along the Pacific coast southward to Chile, and eastward to Argentina. They still make such flights, and the flights are still hazardous, even though the sportsmen have been restrained. Like other small migrating birds, they are vulnerable to storms, and hundreds of them, swept off-course by westerly gales, sometimes arrive in Bermuda. Many others, less fortunate, must simply fail to make any landfall at all.

The snipe, a bird of the wild country, seems to manage much less successfully than woodcock, nighthawk, grouse, or pheasant to get along with humans. We have a few snipe in southern Nova Scotia but they are widely scattered. Unlike the woodcock, they have not taken to nesting in our parks. Unlike the nighthawk, they will not lay eggs on roofs. They do not even seem to frequent farmland, as grouse and pheasants do.

Perhaps it is just as well. When I visit a 'beaver meadow' on some remote part of South Mountain, it is rewarding to hear the wild call of the snipe falling out of the evening sky, and to reflect that this thrilling sound, which the Indians associated with nature spirits, is reserved for those who move at least a short way from the well-beaten tourist trails that run between the ferry terminals and the historic properties of Halifax.

It is quite wrong to assume that human activities are harmful to all wild creatures. Many birds and some mammals are far more numerous than they would be if we failed to modify the environment the way that we do. Robins find lawns and golf courses excellent places to hunt their favourite food, earthworms. The earthworms themselves exist only in small numbers on wild land; they are creatures of cultivation. The weeds and grasses on which pheasants feed become plentiful only when cultivated land begins the long process of returning through successive wild crops to brushland and then to forest. Moose and varying hares both thrive on the young growth that comes up after the pulp companies mow down a stretch of forest. Ruffed grouse find their most plentiful food and cover in lands that have reached a slightly later stage of succession, not in virgin or climax forests. Such animals and birds are favoured by human activities, even if most of them are also hunted.

Land that is cleared and then abandoned provides the ideal habitat for toads, snakes, salamanders, small mammals, and most ground-nesting birds. All such creatures would exist in much smaller numbers if they had to rely on natural clearings and the borders of marshes, or on the few natural meadows that are gradually progressing from lake to forest.

We are an enormously potent force in nature, and we ought to be careful how we act, but turning a patch of woodland into a meadow filled with wild flowers and small mammals and reptiles and birds is not necessarily an evil thing in itself. It's a question of scale. When humans colonized the island of Crete they began to cut down the forests, and continued until even the soil disappeared from the hills. Iceland was once covered with forest, but now has only heathland and grasses. The famous 'cedars of Lebanon,' which provided timber for adjoining nations in the days of King Solomon, not only have disappeared, but have left behind them only rock and dust and goat droppings. North American pioneer farmers, land-clearers, looked upon trees almost as their mortal enemies. In many places they refused even to believe in the value of shelter belts. Today we are in danger of losing our last great forests – and in many places the soil tends to disappear with them, as it did in Lebanon and in Crete. That is the kind of modification to the environment that we had better learn to do without.

4

The Enfolding Hills

Though the tidal flats and salt marshes of the Fundy shore have not changed greatly since the French pioneer Poutrincourt first looked upon them in 1605 and wished to remain here for the rest of his life, the surrounding slopes, our 'mountains,' have changed a great deal. They have not changed much in their shape or their structure. One of them is made of granite, part of the ancient continental plate thrust upward by folding. The other is black lava, much younger, the remains of a long chain of volcanoes that followed an ancient fault line, and have since been worn down from a series of steep cones to a low ridge more than a hundred miles long. Such geological formations change very little in three centuries, but their living community, the forests whose roots rest upon the granite and the lava, have been changed and degraded almost beyond recognition.

For the first three hundred years of European settlement the Annapolis hills were exploited in moderate ways. Men made clearings for small farms, cut logs for timber, hunted and trapped the forest animals. Here and there they destroyed some stretches through the terrible accident of fire, but forests have great regenerative powers. They can recover from fire, if the fire does not come too frequently. The big spruces even have the ability to carry live seeds through a fire and scatter them over the burnt land, where they will germinate. In fact, they will germinate on a burn, but not under litter. Fire is a natural disaster with which the forest has learned to cope. Man-made disasters are another matter. It was not until our own time that the paper companies began chewing the forests into pulp and leaving behind them masses of litter ('slash,' the loggers call it) which may set back the process of regeneration by half a century.

Near the crest of South Ridge, a mile or two from the Annapolis shore, a few tall trees stand out against the sky, huge old spruces towering far above their neighbours, allowed to remain for some strange reason during the destruction in the 1950s of the earlier forest that was mowed down like a field of wheat to feed the maws of the pulp machines. After thirty years, the forest here has just begun to grow back, a mixture of hardwoods and softwoods, firs, and a few spruces and larches. There are some white and red pine seedlings, numerous birches, even some yellow birch, and a few red maples. There are patches of beech, which seem to grow in small stands, all beech together, in spots where the soil happens to favour this tree rather than others. And the ground is beginning to be covered with numerous kinds of shrubs and herbs.

That's what has happened where loggers cut saw logs and firewood, leaving only moderate piles of slash, a little at a time. In other places, where a half-grown forest was clear-felled for pulp, the dense litter left behind has almost stopped the regrowth of trees altogether. Many acres covered with such litter have produced only a tree here and there. The spaces between them, often larger than suburban house lots, are buried under a solid mat of fancy wood ferns, with the taller stems of bracken poking through. The wood ferns will actually grow on the dead wood, and will help, eventually, to convert the litter into soil, in which a new forest will grow. But the whole long process of succession would have been faster by many years if the forest had been burned rather than clear-felled. The hemlock, which grows to enormous size in the few places where it has been left undisturbed, seems to have made little recovery anywhere, either from logging or from pulping. Perhaps it is the last tree of all in the long march of the successive species toward a climax forest.

So long as the present phase of civilization lasts, no climax forest will be allowed to grow again in Nova Scotia. The only exception to this might be a national park, or some small patch of privately owned land. Not only are the paper companies clear-felling the 'second growth' (as they like to call a forest struggling to recover from devastation), but wherever they are allowed to do so they are drenching it with herbicides in an effort to secure pure stands of spruce, which they will then try to keep alive by drenching them with insecticides until the trees are big enough to be mowed down. Those hayfields of unhealthy spruce, awaiting the attacks of budworm, fire, or chain-saw, are pitiful caricatures of healthy climax forests, a few small samples of which can still be seen along the steeper slope of the south ridges, though nothing of the sort has been left between the valley and the sea.

Paper was once a precious commodity. Not until the nineteenth century did it become litter, and not until the twentieth was it manufactured with the express intention that it should become *instant* litter, bound straight for the incinerator to be turned into air pollution. The throw-away culture imposed on Europe and North America by the piracy of 'free enterprise' managed to throw away the great forests of Canada with unbelievable speed. In a single lifetime, my own, they have been reduced from magnificent stands of mature trees, most of them hundreds of years old, to bug-ridden scrub patches, many of which are so unhealthy that they should be burned, in order to allow natural forest succession to begin anew with the red currants and the fire cherries.

Every living thing we touch is turned to stone. Or litter. Or decaying rubbish.

Humans as a species are not such a universal blight as this. We have lived for millions of years on this planet, and have managed, somehow, to be part of its living mantle. Why has western man, pouring out of Spain and France and Britain and Germany and Scandinavia, proved to be such a disaster for all living things? The whales, the seals, the 'game' animals, the fish, the birds, the forests, everything must go, leaving nothing but poisoned crops on poisoned land, and flocks and herds kept alive by antibiotics for a few months until they are ready for the sausage machine. The blight that has spread over the world from western Europe is a horror beyond comprehension.

Nevertheless I marvel at the earth's ability to recover, given half a chance, from our most appalling abuse: those acres of wood ferns are growing in a place where the very soil of South Ridge is buried knee-deep under layers of rotting tree limbs and tops and bark and roots. Even where the topsoil has been bulldozed away, the gold and fire of the hawkweed flourishes, declaring that life will not be put down even by man's most rampant insanity.

We have degraded the whole surface of the world, and are continuing to degrade it. We have degraded the whole structure of life on earth. What we have done to other species is at least as horrifying as what we have done to our own. I'm not at all sure that the German gas ovens or the American nuclear bombing of Japan were any more appalling than the destruction of the buffalo or the extermination of the passenger pigeon.

But the fact that we have done those things does not force us to go on doing them. Only those who wish for a continuation of such evils throw up their hands and call them 'human nature.' Man is a product of his own vision. The visions come first to his prophets, often long before their time, and are often in process of being realized long after their time has passed. We are acting out today the visions of feudal society, visions of knights and personal honour, visions of loyalty to leaders, no matter how wrong-headed; we are also acting out today the visions of a somewhat later time when national states arose, and the ideal of self-sacrifice for the good of the nation supplanted that of loyalty to a feudal lord.

This development, the rise of the nation state, is regarded by the contemporary American essayist Lewis Thomas as 'probably the most stupefying example of biological error since the age of the great reptiles.' But it didn't seem like that when the Mazzinis and the Garibaldis set out to free their people from the tyranny of feuding war-lords.

The people who exterminated the great auks for fish bait and lamp oil were the products of a vision which saw man as top predator in a natural order that was forever red in tooth and claw. It was the same vision that sent the ships of the Hanseatic League questing over the earth seven centuries ago, a vision that perhaps was useful in its time, but became disastrous once its time had passed. As Blake saw all too clearly, Los, the eternal prophet, is a forger of chains.

The people who shovelled Jews and Gypsies into gas ovens were the product of a vision that saw man as a blond Viking mounted on a palamino horse, riding down the lesser breeds with hoof and sword. A remnant of this vision still survives in South Africa. Not every vision has within it the seeds of even transient good. Some visions, even some of those most widely held, can accomplish only evil.

Man is the product of his own vision, and we are capable today of nobler visions than we once were. Most of us no longer regard war as noble, even if large numbers of us are foolish enough to regard it as inevitable, but it was widely regarded as noble a mere two or three generations ago, such a worthy activity, such a high calling, as to be virtually an end in itself. We no longer glorify the slaughter of lesser species. We still kill, and we still fight, but we no longer exalt the killing and the fighting as splendid ends in themselves. Substantial numbers of us have moved beyond the ideal of nation states. Such people stopped the Vietnam War before the genocide became total. We have recently stopped the atrocity of the harp seal massacre off the shores of Canada. Perhaps we can also head off a large-scale nuclear war and the death of civilization.

Many people today have achieved a vision of man as an

animal in which the power of the intellect is wedded to the heart's wisdom and compassion. A few, a *very* few, had such a vision centuries ago. Today it is shared by millions of people; not, certainly, by any majority, but tomorrow, who knows? And in the meantime the vision belongs to those at the growing tip of human evolution. That vision is what man will become. How do I know this? I know it because I will it. I am, myself, at humanity's growing tip. I am of that small fraction of mankind that creates the future, that invents the visions; I spend my life fashioning Adam out of red earth.

Given time – given *enough* time – even the forests will recover. We will outgrow the need for throwaway paper as we outgrew the need for lamp oil. Or we may succeed in removing ourselves from the northern hemisphere by continuing to play with apocalyptic weapons. Or perhaps we will just learn more sense.

One way or another, the devastation will come to an end, and then the budworms will be allowed to prepare the weedy, diseased, artificial forests for the cleansing besom of the fire. And after that the grand parade of successive species toward the calm nobility of the climax forest will begin with the fruit-bearing shrubs and the fire cherries, giving place over the centuries to trees of loftier and slower growth, until at last eastern hemlocks and white pines with bases broader than a man's reach and with spires higher than cathedral towers will stand once more in the places where they stood when the first Europeans sailed along the shores of eastern Canada, and named some part of them Markland (old Norse for 'Forestland') because their most striking feature was the massed ranks of the great evergreen trees.

5

*Blossom
and Renewal*

December is the cruellest month. I recall years at Beachy Cove when roses bloomed outdoors on Christmas Day. There, on the east coast of Newfoundland, February is the cruellest month, and March is its twin, but here the seasons march to a different rhythm. It is not so much that winter arrives in December as that the sun disappears behind the overcast: day after day, week after week, a blanket of cloud obscures the sky, so that I wonder how those hip people celebrated in *Harrowsmith* with their 'total solar houses' would make out here at the end of December. If there's only a dozen hours of sunshine in a month, if the sun doesn't appear even once in three weeks, how does your total solar house get along?

Those are the times when we make use of man's oldest solar storage system, which is still the finest ever invented: dry, hard firewood. Our grandparents relied entirely on such solar storage to heat their houses in winter, and today it is as good as ever – better, perhaps, because we have better stoves and furnaces. In this sense ours, too, is a total solar house. Wood provides truly long-term storage. The energy plucked out of the sky by a tree will not leak away, as it does from a heat sink made of rocks or tanks of water. Unless the tree is allowed to fall and rot on the ground, the solar energy will remain freely available ten years or a hundred years after it is first stored.

We use other forms of storage, too. By late January the shore of Annapolis Basin gets frequent sunshine, and by February 'passive solar heat' provides more warmth than we need. The house faces slightly west of south, with double glazing, lean-to greenhouses on both levels, a lot of brickwork, and flagstone floors for heat sinks. So after a sunny day it will remain warm through most of the night even though the outside temperature may drop to -15^0c. Watching the sun set each day closer and closer to Goat Island is a cheering sight, and helps to make February not a month of gloom at all, but in a sense the first month of spring.

Not only does the sun come back in February, going down in flames day after day behind the great spruces that line the shore between here and Porter's Point, but the sap begins to run visibly in many of the trees and shrubs. You can see the swelling of buds that will not burst into flower and leaf for another two or three months, a slow preparation for the furious activity of early summer when the trees will put on a year's growth in a matter of weeks, and burst almost explosively into flower, followed by the green fruits that will ripen slowly or rapidly, according to their nature, over the rest of the year.

The flowers that will bloom next summer were already starting to form as small buds on the twigs of last July and August, and while the trees have stood, seemingly dead in the snow of midwinter, those buds have been slowly filling with the sap of life that will feed bird and bee with nectar, wasp and man and squirrel with fruit, and will scatter the seeds of another generation of trees across the land.

Already by the last day of January I have brought the first stems of pussy willow indoors to swell into fluffy flowers and prophesy the coming of spring. Children brought them into the schoolrooms every year when I was a child: a time-honoured custom that began, I suppose, when schoolboys were sent out to gather chastising switches, some of which, standing in water to keep them fresh and supple, burst into flower, and thenceforth were kept to fill young eyes with beauty instead of with tears.

Already the potted potentilla, which shed its last bloom and its last leaf in November, is clothing itself in pale green, content with its two-month rest, and is sending out minute flower buds for the new year. Almost unable to believe it is happening so soon, I pick one of them, dissect it under a magnifying glass, and there, sure enough, are the yellow anthers, surrounded by the first sprouts of petals, all wrapped in a sheath about the size of a grain of rice. So January ends with cheer and promise; the year is beginning to renew itself; the gloom of December is well and truly past.

The first spring we lived here we arrived at the end of March, and camped in the small shed that we had built the autumn before while living in a tent. While living in the shed we built the house. It had been a warm month of March, but April arrived with frost, and even a spatter of snow. Then one morning Andrew, aged four, came rushing in to announce that he had found a flower. We all went off to see it, and there it was, miraculous in the grass, the first violet.

'Don't pick it, Leah!' he ordered his two-year-old sister (not that she would have, she insists). Two weeks later we'd be eating violets in a salad, for at the peak of the season the land turned purple with them, but this one was sacrosanct, the first flower of spring.

Later that day Corky came in from exploring the woods to announce, 'There's a shrub in the ravine, all out in bloom.' We couldn't believe it, for it was still winter. A violet we could credit, but a flowering shrub! Everything looked dead, not a leaf in sight, not a bud showing green. We had never heard of the purple-flowered laurel, the Mediterranean Daphne brought here so many generations ago. We went to see it, and there it was, a winter miracle, not only draped like a lilac, but drenched in heavenly fragrance. We discovered much later that this remarkable little shrub, blooming about a month earlier than any of the native flowering trees, had naturalized and run wild through all the woods of our region. It grows only three or four feet high, and keeps to sheltered, semi-shaded places, so you never see it while walking along a road or through a field. Many of our neighbours have never heard of its existence. A place in thick woods where a little sunlight penetrates through a hole in the canopy is the favourite haunt of the Daphne, and only those walking through the woods at the beginning of April are likely to see it in bloom. At any other time it is a nondescript sprig of a plant on which no one would waste a second glance.

Violets and Daphne are not our earliest wildflowers. Earlier still, earlier than the garden snowdrops and crocuses, the coltsfoot comes into bloom. We saw none that first spring, but found it later at Clementsport and transplanted some of it to a gravel bank with a southern slope where almost nothing else would grow. It soon spread to cover this bit of waste ground, and now it comes into bloom every year before the end of March. For us the coltsfoot is truly the first flower of spring, blooming in profusion, producing thousands of yellow daisies a full month before the dandelions. But the coltsfoot is a more interesting flower than any dandelion. It blooms before it sends up its leaves, on short curved stems covered with pink scales. The yellow flowers, too, are backed with pink, and when they fade they are followed by tufts of down, but the principal charm of the coltsfoot is its earliness: it spreads a splash of yellow colour over a rocky slope or a pile of talus before anything else is in bloom. After the flower and seed, the broad leaves unfold, quite attractive in themselves, rather like the kind of fig leaves seen on Victorian copies of Greek statues. This hardy pioneer will cover waste banks, even the shoulders of crushed stone along highways, where almost nothing will grow, clothing the bare rock with blossoms for a week or two, and with attractive verdure for the rest of the spring and summer.

About a month after the Daphne fades the serviceberries burst into bloom. How much better is the Newfoundland name chuckly pear! Serviceberry indeed! And how much uglier the

American name, shadbush! But whatever you call them, their blooming is a high point of the year. At Annapolis there are several species, some of them small shrubs, others growing into trees twenty-five feet tall. When they bloom in mid-May the woods on every side are dressed in great veils of pink and white, for though all the flowers are white, some species have pink sepals, and leaves that are red when they first unfold. The great drifts of blossoms fill every dark space along the edges of the woods. I have never seen any forest anywhere more beautiful with bloom than the Annapolis woodlands in May during the brief flowering of the chuckly pears.

Later, the children will gather the fruit, almost live on it while it is at its peak, and perhaps I'll even turn a gallon or so of the purple berries into wine, but the fruit is nothing compared to the flowers – indeed, the big trees that bloom most handsomely seem to produce few berries; it is as though they were producing a feast for bees and for human eyes rather than labouring to distribute seed.

The chuckly pears were one of the attractions that brought us to Annapolis Basin. They were in bloom in 1978 when we came here and camped, first at Smith's Cove, then at Upper Clements, exploring the area with the idea of finding a home-site. We were so attracted by the beauties of the basin and the adjoining woods, at their very best when we first saw them, that we went into a real estate office and bought an option on the land, and paid the balance a month later. What a fortunate choice it was!

As the chuckly pears fade, the pin cherries begin to bloom, then the black cherries, and last of all the chokecherries. While this is happening the marsh marigolds spread their brilliant yellow through the ravine, and red, white, and pink trilliums blossom under the trees. About this time, too, the cockspur thorn (our commonest native hawthorn) comes out in clumps of creamy white, a round-headed bush with attractive leaves and fruits as well as flowers. But you'd better respect the three-inch thorns! The haws are edible, but only the birds eat them.

The wild hedgerows are home to trailing arbutus – mayflower, as it is called here, very delicate and beautiful, and incidentally one of the few broad-leafed evergreens native to Nova Scotia. The edges of the woods are filled with blackberries and roses. Besides the native wild roses we have at least three species of roses from Europe and Asia that have run wild. One of them, the white eglantine, forms a large, round shrub buried in blossoms, as elegant and ornamental as any shrub you can buy from a nursery. The brambles and briers bloom in succession, and in late summer the brambles add a crop of delicious berries in extravagant abundance.

The second year we lived here we decided to stop mowing our meadow (which till then had produced nothing but hay), confining our grass-cutting to about two acres of wild lawn. The rest we turned over to birds and animals and insects, and it promptly grew into a wildflower garden, merging downhill into a cranberry marsh, and producing a perpetual succession of bloom throughout spring, summer, and autumn.

After the violets come the blue-eyed grass, delightful little irises only four or five inches high, but often growing in clusters. Then big clumps of blue-flag iris bloom at the same time as the fancy bearded iris in our flower border. The gorgeous blue flags require nothing except living space and lots of water, and will continue to bloom year after year for centuries so long as the space is not overgrown by taller plants. With no help from us they have completely surrounded one of our ponds. Lovely purple loosestrife, another import from Europe, is beginning to bloom there, too.

By early summer the meadow has numerous spikes of pink-purple fringed orchids, the flower heads four or five inches long, with a heady perfume equal to that of any garden flower that grows. Underneath the shrubs there will be small patches of yellow honeysuckle, only a foot or so high, and, like the Daphne, requiring shade. Along the path clumps of wild columbine nod in the wind.

The field daisies, ox-eye daisies as they are often called,

spread everywhere, especially over land that has recently been allowed to lie fallow after cultivation. I have to wonder why we bother to grow shasta daisies when the field daisy is just like it, and so much more plentiful. The shasta is a shade larger, it is true, and blooms a bit later, but these differences don't seem important enough to make the shastas worth the trouble. The wild daisy, like its yellow cousin the black-eyed Susan, will provide acres of bloom if given the space, flowering with the red clover in a veritable sea of red, white, and yellow.

In midsummer, along the edge of the land above the beach, the pink morning glories and the red roses create a riot of blossoms, climbing over piles of rotting seaweed, burying grass and shrubs, filling the ground with colour and the air with perfume.

The lupines, acres and square miles of them, bloom in June, eye-catching masses of red, white, pink, and blue, with dashes of yellow, and rich shades of imperial purple, but the humble little ground ivy spreads its indigo carpet from May to September, complementing the hawkweed and the St. John's wort in nature's favourite blend of colours, purple and gold. Mustard and purple vetch provide another such combination. Later in the season there is still another, the goldenrod and the dusty asters (or Michaelmas daisies), which grow here in mounds up to six feet tall. In a good year the asters bury themselves in blossoms of lilac and purple. Goldenrod provides the last great burst of bloom before the blaze of the autumn leaves, and the bees work frantically gathering its nectar to fill their hives for winter. In England, where goldenrod doesn't grow wild, people plant it in their gardens.

Our meadow now serves a far nobler end than that of the hayfield it used to be. From April to October it is home to a splendid succession of flowering plants that provide food and shelter for numberless active creatures great and small, from tiny gnats to lordly pheasants. Hummingbirds visit it every day in summer, delighted especially with the lovely jewelweed that holds out its orange-coloured baskets of flowers, offering its gift of nectar to butterflies and birds.

Beneath its canopy of leaves and flowers the meadow is home to hundreds, perhaps thousands, of small animals, to toads and snakes and jumping mice, to voles that scurry among its roots, making small tunnels that meet and intersect like highways, and to shrews and moles that hide underground. But perhaps most important of all, if you are interested in gardening, it is home to a thousand species of insects, including a veritable army of predatory wasps and flies. The predators are mostly tiny things not much bigger than mosquitoes, but they do a very big job by preventing the explosion of pest insects among our crops.

Our only experience of a serious attack by an insect pest began in 1983 with an invasion of forest tent caterpillars. This is one of two species of tent caterpillar common in our area, the other being the orchard tent caterpillar. One of the differences between the two is that the forest species does not build the dense webs that we call tents, but it attacks orchard trees, blueberry shrubs, ornamentals, just about everything, once it has finished gobbling its favourite food, the leaves of the two species of aspen, which it strips bare.

We had been destroying a few tents of the orchard tent caterpillars for three years, finding them mostly in cherries and wild apples in our woods, as well as among our peaches, but we were in no way prepared for what happened one day in early June when I looked out the window and saw a denuded aspen standing among the leafy trees in our ravine. Investigating, we found millions of caterpillars on the aspen trunks, patches of them in dense swarms heading for the leaves. Their strategy is to eat the leaves of one tree, then drop down to the ground and set off like Mongol hordes through the forest litter for the next. We found that we could reach most of them by hand or with sticks. So Corky, Andrew, Leah, and I spent the next three days squashing tent caterpillars into green mush. It was disgusting work, but we saved our trees from defoliation. Only three or four of them were totally stripped of leaves in a year when square miles of wild woodland were denuded. By estimating the numbers to each tree, and the numbers of trees that we cleaned, we concluded that we had destroyed more than a hundred million of the insects.

The aspens recovered, and the maples and birches remained untouched. But many thousands of the caterpillars built cocoons wherever they could find an elevated crevice – along the eaves of our house, for instance. The children brought some of them indoors, and fed them in glass jars, where they eventually pupated and emerged as moths. By examining some dozens of the chrysalides I discovered that many of them had been attacked and killed by a parasite.

'I think we're in luck,' I told Corky. 'After such a population explosion there's bound to be a crash. The pupating moths seem to be heavily parasitized.'

'I hope so,' she said. 'They're horrible creatures. I think I'd hate anything that swarmed like that.'

Because it builds its cocoon right in the open, the tent caterpillar is a sitting duck for a flying parasite. The parasite can easily find its prey and bore a hole right into the tempting storehouse of caterpillar meat.

It was such a hopeful sign that we were quite unprepared for what happened the next year. I was busy clipping off and burning the tents of orchard tent caterpillars in the early summer of 1984 when I looked across our meadow into the ravine and saw the trunks of every aspen blackened with crawling insects – ten times more of the forest tent caterpillars than there had been the year before. The ground was a crawling mass of them. Where there had been hundreds of millions, there were now billions.

We made long-poled torches dipped in buckets of used crankcase oil, and burned and smoked them out of as many of the trees as we could. We saved a few dozen trees from defoliation. But that year our woods was denuded. After a week it looked like a midwinter scene, a tangle of bare branches. I decided to try painting all the trunks with used oil as soon as I saw the next invasion beginning. I'm still not sure if that would stop them and I'm glad I haven't had to try it.

That was the year they attacked our orchard and our ornamental shrubs. We managed to prevent the trees from being eaten, but then millions of full-grown caterpillars arrived from the woods, and wrapped themselves in the leaves to pupate. Every leaf on our flowering almond, for example, was curled into a knot, glued together by cocoons. Corky spent a week uncurling leaves and picking out the pupae from fruit trees and ornamentals.

Then our denuded woods began putting out a gallant second crop of leaves. Only the few trees that had been denuded the year before, then denuded again a second, failed to recover. By the end of July our small forest was a sea of verdure once more. Most trees will survive a single defoliation, but may be killed if it happens twice in a year, or two years running.

However, while all this was happening something else was happening, too, unseen and unsuspected. I began picking the cocoons from the crevices of the house in handfuls. Examining them, I found that every single one had a small hole in it. Inside, the pupating insect was eaten out to a mere husk. I searched through hundreds of them without finding a live grub. Clearly, the parasites had exploded in a vast population boom a year behind the explosion of their prey, the caterpillars. The grubs we had failed to kill the year before had provided food for many thousands of growing parasites. Now perhaps a million parasites were scouring the area looking for a place to deposit their eggs, and the caterpillars in their cocoons were being wiped out.

'This time I really believe they've been knocked down,' I told Corky. 'I can't find a live one anywhere.'

'I hope so,' she said. 'Just the same, you'd better be ready with the oil next year.'

But there was no need for the oil next year. I'm pleased that this outstanding example of biological control happened on my own land, under my own nose. If, like the government of New

Brunswick, we had resorted to poison spray, we would have destroyed the parasites, and, like the misguided forest managers, we would have been locked into a permanent battle, year after year, with nothing to look forward to but poisoned forest and poisoned land henceforth and forever. Fortunately, the thought of mass poisoning never once crossed our minds.

I have never seen such a classic example of an uncontrollable population explosion followed by a total population crash. The year after the apparent disaster, and the year after that, there wasn't a forest tent caterpillar to be found anywhere. Not only that, but the orchard tent caterpillars had disappeared too. Not a tent in sight. Presumably the parasite that had fed on the forest tent caterpillars had wiped out the orchard species as well. We are now enjoying our third caterpillar-free year.

As a result we have a healthy bit of young and growing forest that becomes lovelier year by year. At least fifty species of birds build their nests in and among the trees. Varying hares flourish, and girdle enough of the young aspens a foot or two above the ground to thin them properly, making space for maples and birches, which the hares ignore. Wild holly colours the forest, and bayberry scents its air. The larches and the spruces stretch skyward from its glades. Everything from the bark beetle to the white-tailed deer is at home there, even the caterpillar, somewhere unseen, waiting to explode once more into a plague. Fortunately the little parasite is there too, our friend and the friend of the forest, waiting to drive the tent caterpillar back to its proper place as a modest member of the forest community.

Because we have provided an ample home for predatory insects, snakes, toads, and other insectivores, including birds, and because this wild land surrounds our cultivated gardens, we have had almost no trouble from pests, and have had no need whatever for insecticides. We have never used even an 'organic' insecticide on any crop, and have never suffered serious damage. Our gardens supply all our needs for vegetables – far more, indeed, than we can eat in our small nuclear family, the only expense, except for a few gallons of gasoline for the tractor, being the money we spend on seed.

The wild meadow provides certain aesthetic enjoyments over and above its numerous flowers. Many of the small predatory insects that live there are among the most beautiful products of organic evolution. As I write this, one of them is walking beneath my desk lamp beside my typewriter. Its wings are pure gold – not yellow, but shining, metallic gold. Others gleam like emeralds, reflecting the light. Many of them are truly living jewels among the wildflowers, though so small that they are rarely seen except by those with the time and patience to look at nature in fine detail as well as in vast extent.

6

Of Worms and Men

As our first winter at Annapolis passed into spring we began using up all the potting soil that we had mixed the autumn before, setting out flats of seeds, and pricking out the seedlings into more flats. We knew from the day we arrived that this was a place where we were going to grow every vegetable and fruit common to the north temperate zone, and, with the enthusiasm of someone whose gardening has been severely restricted in the past, Corky began growing not dozens, but *hundreds* of tomato plants, peppers, eggplants, all the common members of the cabbage family, all the popular root crops, peas, beans, lettuce, corn, and so on. Hence the need for potting soil.

Fortunately there were a couple of bushels of ordinary topsoil sitting in the cellar, where I had thoughtfully stored them four months earlier. I now proceeded to mix this with peat moss, limestone, bone meal, and a few handfuls of dried sheep manure. The stored soil was as dry as Portland cement, making it all the easier to sift out the stones. But as I began sifting this loam-turned-to-dust I discovered to my amazement that it contained not only stones, but live earthworms that had survived a winter-long estivation without water.

The remarkable thing was that each earthworm had tied itself into a complex series of overhand knots so that it presented the smallest possible surface to the moisture-absorbing dried loam while retaining a few vital drops of water inside the tight bundle of its knotted coils. Here was a survival technique that would permit the earthworm to live through a prolonged drought, then to revive and reproduce with the coming of the rain. I had to marvel at such sophisticated behaviour in a creature as humble as a worm, all the more remarkable because the habit had survived in a population of earthworms that had probably not experienced a natural drought during the current geological era. A drought requiring earthworms to estivate has probably not occurred in this part of the world since the ranges of hills acquired their present shape and the layer of topsoil was laid down. Those worms had 'remembered,' from untold generations ago, how to survive in a desert.

'Look at this,' I said to Corky, showing her a worm that looked dead until you began untying it.

'I've never seen anything like it. How do you suppose it happened?'

We soaked the worm and put it on a patch of damp soil and watched it 'come back to life.' Then we began discussing the nature of instinct, and the techniques of information storage. The habit could only be preserved in the DNA molecule, we were sure – but that left a lot to be explained, for somehow the simple code of the nucleotides preserves not only the information needed to build organs, but complex patterns of habit and behaviour, and manages to preserve this information in cold storage, while it is not needed, over very long spans of time.

'I suppose all earthworms curl up to conserve moisture,' Corky conjectured.

'Yes, I'm sure, and when it's very dry they no doubt curl more and more tightly. But knots? A series of overhand knots, forming a ball?'

'Could it happen by accident?'

'Yes, I suppose so, the first time. But see, they've all done it. It's not an accident now.'

This accident, if accident it was, happened often enough to develop into an instinct, a strong enough, sufficiently well-fixed instinct to survive through thousands of generations in a wet climate.

'The whole thing seems extremely unlikely. But how else would an earthworm know what to do?'

I'm what people call a neo-Darwinist. Though I think Darwin went a long way toward explaining what happened as life developed on earth, I think he did less well trying to explain *how* it happened and *why* it happened. His insistence on accident rings false. Darwin had lifelong doubts about this himself, and was driven to extreme positions in defence of his theory that evolution moves forward solely by the survival of lucky accidents. Lucky accidents, happening purely by chance, in a completely random way, may help to shape new species. But, together with many other naturalists, I don't believe they explain everything, or even evolution's main drive.

Of course I have no doubt at all about evolution as a historic and continuing process. I'm as sure as I am of anything I know that this is a process basic to the entire physical universe. But it seems to me that a great deal about how evolution operates in the contemporary world (the world of the last few million years) has yet to be explained. In some way that is not clear, the environment must affect the organism so as to produce special adaptations much more rapidly than can be explained by the mere accretion of lucky accidents. Darwin was not a mathematician. Even if he had been, he would not have been able to work out the number of chance happenings needed to turn a scale into a feather, or a fin into a foot. Only with knowledge of the scale involved in each step, of the frequency of accidents, and only with a computer to do the arithmetic, can we get even a rough idea of the time involved, and it turns out to be thousands of times longer than Darwin supposed. In Darwin's time it seemed that *anything* might happen in a few million generations, millions being numbers that boggled the human imagination. But computers handle such numbers in the blink of an eye, and using computers we can now say for certain that turning a toad into an eagle ought to take billions, not mere millions, of years.

I'm amazed that people can look at what happened to the Darwin finches, one of the most convincing demonstrations of evolution in action, and fail to marvel at the speed with which new forms have appeared.

How long since the Galapagos Islands rose above *and remained above* the sea? Only so long as volcanoes still active have been erupting. The islands were there through the last short ice age (when they were one island instead of an archipelago) and, as mere peaks peeping above the water, through at least a part of the preceding interglacial period. Before that? Darwin believed that the islands had been 'always' there, isolated from the mainland, and from each other, so that limitless stretches of time were available to develop their unique species. Now we know that this was not so. The oldest lava on the Galapagos is about two million years old, but was probably laid down under water. The islands' continuous existence above sea level is probably much less than that, and their existence as separate island entities less still. And yet, in the relatively few generations available to it, a single species of finch has been able to turn itself into a dozen different kinds of bird ranging from 'flycatcher' to 'woodpecker.' If one accidental mutation in a thousand turned out to be lucky, and a thousand lucky mutations were assembled end to end, you might get a woodpecker from a finch. But for that to happen in a million generations, there'd have to be at least one mutation in every nest. So we can say for certain that something not yet observed produces the 'lucky' mutations far more often than mere chance might dictate, and this something, whatever it may turn out to be, lies at the very core of organic evolution, explaining the otherwise inexplicable: how it happened that the earth became populated with such an incredible variety of life in such a geologically short period.

'God,' said Albert Einstein, 'doesn't play dice with the

universe.' He was arguing against the commonly accepted interpretation of quantum theory, but he might equally well have been arguing about biology. And in either case, he might have been wrong. For games of chance, in fact, are quite predictable if you play them long enough, and god, if he plays dice, has been playing a long time (as I discuss in Appendix B).

The great physicist Wolfgang Pauli was sceptical about Darwin's theory that biological evolution happened solely because of the accretion of lucky accidents, and pointed out its mathematical implausibility. I mention Pauli because no one will doubt the power of his intellect or the rigour of his science. If he was sceptical of a scientific dogma, his scepticism is not to be taken lightly (as my own might be).

It seems to me that two fundamental errors may be at work: first, the totally false but very common belief that chance is additive, cumulative; second, a basic, but so far unexplained, flaw in the laws of probability. The flaw can be demonstrated empirically, though we cannot explain its nature. Every poker player uses the mathematics of chance. If he does not know the odds, then he has learned to use them from experience. If he is a successful poker player he also 'plays his rushes,' the periods when the laws of chance seem to be suspended. Such rushes, like hot dice in a crap game, are far too well established to be dismissed as imaginary. Any player who ignores them goes broke. They are sometimes 'explained' as a psychic phenomenon, but the explanation seems inadequate to me because the rushes still happen when the cards are shuffled and dealt by a machine, and I find it hard to credit that a player's emotional excitement can make a machine deal him a straight flush. It seems far simpler to believe, as I do, that the mathematics of chance is imperfectly understood, that it is not as simple as our elementary logic would lead us to believe. But in any case the point is that the rushes *do* occur.

I believe there are rushes in biology as well as in games of chance, and that evolving species play their rushes well-nigh infallibly. Maybe god doesn't place dice with the universe, but

I'm willing to bet that he plays poker.

Among most people who have turned their minds to the problems of evolution there has been a major misunderstanding of the mathematics of chance and large numbers. (Few of them have been even amateur mathematicians.) Chance is not cumulative, like arsenic. Quite the contrary. The more you have of it, the less there is. In one throw of the die it is pure chance what number comes up. But in six million throws the six will come up a million times – not two million, or half a million, but a million times. *Large numbers cancel chance*. They do it in biology just as they do it in physics. There is no way we can predict when, if ever, an atom of uranium-235 will decay, or when two or three or four of them will decay, if ever. But if we have ten billion such atoms, we can say with absolute certainty that five billion of them will decay in seven hundred million years.

It happens in biology as surely as it happens in quantum mechanics, or in dice-throwing. The effect is to give evolution a direction, an inevitability, which seems so uncanny that many people have been driven to postulate a mysterious life force, an *élan vital*, pushing evolution in a chosen direction. But when you really understand that chance, multiplied by itself often enough, produces not more chance but the inevitable, then the mystery disappears. And in biology the numbers are very, very large indeed. In any one species you are likely to have millions, even billions, of individuals, all of whose ancestors have passed through millions or billions of generations.

Life is chemistry carried toward its logical conclusion. This simple truth was not understood until very recently. Instead of making life less miraculous, it makes chemistry more wonderful. In a sense, life must have been inherent in matter from the moment it condensed out of the energy front of the 'big bang.' It used to be assumed that life was a lucky accident, a billion-to-one chance that happened against all odds and only once. We now know that this was a purely romantic notion, a belief rooted in our former ignorance of complex chemistry and the evolution of matter in its pre-living stages. We can now detect organic chemicals almost everywhere, even in 'empty' space, and we know that high levels of chemical evolution take place in the neighbourhood of every star. This widespread occurrence of organic chemicals throughout the universe has led us to believe, in turn, that they will continue to evolve into living chemicals whenever and wherever they can. The process seems to have the same kind of inevitability as starshine. Stars do not have to be turned on by a lucky accident. They turn themselves on wherever a sufficiently large amount of the universal matter comes together in one place. And wherever a mass of materials of the right size comes together into a planet at the right distance from a star, the universal matter of that planet will evolve more and more complex levels of chemistry until it reaches that level of complexity that we call 'life.'

It used to be assumed that life could have evolved on earth only once. Even after the mystery of its evolution had been explained, people kept inventing reasons to believe that it was a unique event. Among such suggestions was the conjecture that the first living molecule gobbled up every complex molecule around it, like a cancer spreading through an organ, so that the possibility of a second life event was denied. This, too, we now see to be a romance, an invention of the human mind, a gratification of our appetite for the marvellous. In all likelihood life evolved on earth not once, but millions or billions of times. Why, then, does all life have the same basic chemistry? The answer to this is straightforward, too: it is likely that only one form of living chemistry is *possible*.

Thus, too, I am led to question the widely held belief that life evolved only in the sea, and that it 'emerged from the sea' at a late period. It is absolutely certain that a number of complex creatures emerged from the sea, not once, but time and again. All large land animals seem to be descended from marine ancestors. What is not certain is that the land was lifeless before their arrival. I think it quite likely that life evolved on land as well as in the sea, that numerous kinds of bacteria-like plants may have been able to survive in favoured places before the land was ready to support complex organisms, and that they may well have evolved as far as they could within the limits of the severe conditions prevailing, long before the first arthropod crawled out on a mud flat and dried itself in the sun. There was probably primitive food already waiting on land when the first complex creatures emerged from the sea. That, rather than the mere urge to expand into an empty space, was perhaps the principal motive behind the migration.

If life is not a lucky accident, if it happens wherever it can, if it follows not a chance path of chemical evolution, but the only path that is possible, then there is no need to 'explain' why all life on earth is so similar, or refer it all to a single original miraculous molecule. And if this is so, then it is very likely indeed that life evolved in terrestrial caves and lakes, and even in marshes, wherever it might be shielded from the hard radiation falling out of a sky not yet containing a protective layer of ozone. Such evolution could have been independent of evolution in the sea. We have every reason to believe that wherever the development took place it progressed as far as it could within the limits imposed by the surrounding conditions.

I should not have to say (but perhaps I do) that none of this is a denial of the miraculous. Far from it. The more we understand the universe, and the more we comprehend the inevitability of the way it works, the more miraculous it becomes. A star coming to birth from wandering clouds of gas and dust, a redwood tree born from starshine, a dolphin leaping out of a seething mass of reacting chemicals, are far grander miracles, miracles of an altogether higher and more awesome order, than the simple sorcerer's trick of the old man in the nightgown moulding Adam out of mud and setting him going by mouth-to-mouth breathing.

As for the human animal, and human evolution (you expected this, I'm sure, since, like me, you're a member of the most narcissistic species on the face of the earth), I have a paragraph to spare for that, too:

Humans are not perfect and not perfectible. Humanity is one

expression of evolution; we belong in this time and at this level, and within those limits we are a very potent force in the flow of life. Humans have demonstrated enormous potential, much of it probably still unrealized. We may have a long way to go before we reach our full flowering. We may be capable of achievements still undreamed. Nevertheless, the human species is limited and mortal. Its destiny is not to populate the universe but to achieve as much awareness and effectiveness in this solar system as it possibly can before getting out of the way of the more effective species that will come later. The idea that evolution has been working, from the beginning, toward this particular animal, and that its final flowering will be achieved in this single species, is too naïve to be considered.

I must add, though, that I do not share the anti-human attitudes of such major naturalists as Farley Mowat and Loren Eiseley. Mowat, like Eiseley before him, sees mainly the evil in mankind. Eiseley, who did nearly all of his writing in the last twenty years of his life, tended to confuse his own decline with a despair inherent in his species. Such confusion is common among writers. The last gift to the world by H. G. Wells was a long essay on the human mind at the end of its tether, written just before we began to use computers and to venture out among the stars. Of course it was Wells who had reached the end of his tether, not humanity.

There's little doubt that the present human species will in time become degenerate, overaged, and decrepit. Just now it is in the full flush of its youth, deeply charged with life, humming with the currents of both good and evil, immensely dangerous to other life forms, but immensely full of promise, too. To bury humanity among the fallen leaves and invoke the Fifth Great Glaciation, as Eiseley did in the last years of his life, is to wallow in the romanticism of despair.

Many things contributed to Eiseley's despair. He was well aware that he had wasted much of his life as a university teacher, and misspent much more of it digging for bones, when his true vocation was accumulating and transmitting wisdom.

Trying always to be a naturalist, marvelling at the miraculous devices of life, he lived, nevertheless, in a great city where the seeds of life were smothered by concrete and asphalt. He failed to reflect that all the cities of the world occupy far less than one per cent of its surface, and that the health of the planet is not to be judged by the ill-health of the City of New York.

Naturalist-philosophers are especially liable to despair. Some, like Thoreau, experience it in their lives, but do not transmit it in their writing. Thoreau was especially disappointed by the human condition, which not only fell far short of his ideal, but came close to utterly opposing it. But Thoreau had the strength of character that most writers lack. The quality that he set against despair was courage, and it was from this standpoint that he wrote. He had a lofty concept of the writer's mission: 'We should impart our courage and not our despair,' he said. When he had no more courage to impart, he turned from the human condition to writing about simpler things.

If we could really get an outside, objective view of the earthly biosphere, I believe it would look quite different from the view we see on the inside. I suspect our own importance would dwindle. Humans are not, by any means, the only marvel created by the evolution of life on earth. Everything we see around us is the end product of billions of years of evolutionary change. When we look at a long-horned beetle or a red eft, for example, each a highly interesting member of its order – an exceptionally ornamental insect, an exquisitely beautiful amphibian – we may be tempted to think of them as 'primitive' creatures. They are not. Evolution has been working toward the production of the beetle, the eft, the silver birch, and the human being for exactly the same length of time. Life has flowered in multitudinous ways, all of them complex, and to describe any of the end products of evolution as 'primitive' is to make a simplistic value judgment similar to that made by white racists who class as 'primitive' humans with brown skins.

Who on earth decreed that intelligence should be life's

highest expression? The answer is obvious. Male humans decreed it, and especially those who write books. If books were written by caribou stags, life's highest expression might be regarded as a fine spread of antlers. Antlers are the stag's specialty, just as intelligence is ours.

A house cat has more intelligence than a hermit thrush. Is the song of the house cat therefore superior? An ant has more brains than a hemlock. Is the ant therefore a 'higher' form of life?

Life has produced many wonders besides intelligence, and they cannot be ranked in a hierarchy. Leaving intelligence completely aside for the moment, let's ask which is 'higher,' the scent of the white water lily or the song of the hermit thrush? Since neither of those two superb expressions of creative evolution points in the human direction, we are less likely to be prejudiced when we compare them than when we compare a dragonfly and a mouse, for example. The mouse clearly points toward the human. And the fact that I prefer the dragonfly, that I feel a true sense of love for this marvellous winged creature, demonstrates how perversely far I have strayed from the normal human viewpoint.

We are shamelessly parochial when we draw our diagrams showing the branches of the evolutionary tree. The plants are not on the main stem. Fish, amphibians, and reptiles all got off to an earlier start than mammals, and are shown growing off to one side. Because mammals came late, we feel justified in placing them on a higher branch than those other branches of the animal kingdom. But the real reason we do it is that we are mammals ourselves. Before we even started our chart we had decided that *Homo sapiens* was going to be at the tip of the main stem.

The reptiles did not stop evolving when the first mammal appeared. Nor did the first amphibian put an end to the evolution of fishes. The birds are a bit of an embarrassment. It isn't at all certain that the first bird was flying before the first mammal rooted in the mud. Wouldn't it be just terrible to discover that some branches of the animal kingdom have evolved more recently than our own?

It happens, too, that our mammalian ancestors were scuttling among the ferns before the first flower burst into bloom. The branch of the flowering plants is a recent budding of the tree of life, more recent than ours. Are they a higher expression of life's true essence?

Well, if youth isn't to be the standard for measuring the highest forms of life, and if intelligence isn't to be the standard, then what? Let me suggest beauty. That would put some of the insects right up there beside the flowers, and I'm not sure just where we'd come in. Or plain, old-fashioned *success*? What could be more human than that standard? It would put the Norwegian rat a long way ahead of the gorilla, though perhaps not quite on a level with ourselves. And, of course, the cockroach would get a high rating, too.

It is often said that humans are the only truly unspecialized animals, that we have 'escaped the trap of specialization,' that this indeed constitutes our uniqueness among the many millions of species of the earth's inhabitants. Well, what are those pages of squiggles that we worship, those cryptic sets of equations that we profess to believe are revealed truth? What are they, and the over-developed left brain that they represent, if not the most extreme specialization in the living world?

The over-specialized fangs of the sabre-toothed tiger. The overgrown antlers of the Irish elk. The over-developed left hemispheres of human reductionists.

I'd class the brown rat, among mammals, as comparatively unspecialized. The raven among birds. The green algae among plants.

But humans may be the most specialized, and perhaps the most 'trapped,' of all terrestrial creatures. We have become more and more dependent on our ability to program computers. What would happen, after a thousand years of such dependency, if a change of environment made it impossible to generate or store electric power?

What the horns did to the Irish elk the left brain is clearly threatening to do to the human animal. Extreme specialization is indeed a dangerous road, often with a dead end.

In Europe there was once a tradition that every scholar must also learn a trade. It was a deliberate attempt to prevent over-specialization, to keep even the intellectual priesthood in touch with reality. It would be a very good idea indeed if we followed a similar plan, if our universities refused to grant degrees to able-bodied men and women until the applicants could grow potatoes, build boats, repair simple machines, or survive a week in the woods. In many situations the ability to fell and cleave firewood vastly outclasses the ability to read differential equations. It doesn't require a nuclear winter. I've been there myself, caught out on a Labrador lake in a canoe and forced to spend the night on an island in a snowstorm – a night I spent in relative comfort because I knew how to build a big fire, even in bad weather. No one ought to forget the basic human skills that our ancestors developed in the Old Stone Age, or even earlier. Retaining such skills would help to prevent the drift into over-specialization that could put an end to us all.

We are the first animal with intelligence enough to destroy itself by the mere misuse of its brains. If we do it (and I am not one who believes we are going to), let's hope that we don't drag down the whole terrestrial biosphere with us. Without human intervention the plants might continue to evolve even more marvellous expressions of life than those they have already produced.

It isn't man that is the great miracle of our solar system. It is the whole evolving biosphere of which he is a part, of which, perhaps, he could be the 'brain' if he could learn enough humility to realize that the brain, by itself, is nothing: a mass of helpless tissue totally and utterly dependent upon all the other living components of the organism.

And so, to come back to our earthworms, after our long detour through space and time: Humble as they seem, they too are a miracle, and not only because they can tie themselves into knots. They fit into the living community of the soil with the same kind of perfection, the same kind of lock-and-key relationship, as the clover and the bee fit into the community of the meadow. They contribute vastly to the welfare of all living creatures, from microbes to men, and have evolved with them, as the soil evolved, from its first primitive structure of mineral dust to its present complexity teeming and bursting with life and fertility. They, too, are the product of billions of years of evolution, travelling with us through the solar system, travelling with the solar system through the galaxy, travelling with the galaxy through the universe on the greatest of all journeys, a living part of a living planet, one of a host of such in the universal family of the stars.

7

Fire Dance

I have seen the willets dancing in the springtime on the shore, dancing not only on the short salt grass that is covered monthly by the tide, but dancing in air, like butterflies, or salamanders wrapped in flame. This three-dimensional dance, a spiral reaching toward the sky, expands and replicates the helix that is at the core of life: the double spiral of the chromosome, the protean spirals of the albuminoids, the simplicity and perfection of the circle with the added dimensions of motion and time, the elements that make of all perfection a transience, a flowering, and a becoming.

Such is the dance of these feathered spirits; they move in rhythmic measures through the radiance that glimmers from the waves, as twin planets might move, each orbiting the other about their common centre, then rise like twirling smoke, still orbiting, and quiver at perihelion before returning to the earth to complete the dance with intertwined circles once more, a quadrilateral symmetry, adorned at both ends with simple but decorative motifs, like a minuet or a scherzo.

Arthur Cleveland Bent, who devoted himself to writing the *Life Histories of the Birds of North America* (and actually completed a good deal of it before he died), took part in many a mass shooting of shorebirds, chopped up many a carcass, and poked around in the half-digested mess of many a willet's last meal to study its 'food habits.' But he never saw willets dancing, as I have seen them, or knew them in the way I know them, not as 'things' to be described and reported, but as companions in life's adventure. I have seen a willet at little more than arm's length sitting on her four mottled eggs knowing full well that I was not an agent of death, but an ambassador from one of life's neighbouring countries. By walking humbly in the world, and treating its living inhabitants with respect, you can learn far more about their true nature than Bent and Audubon and other disciples of Newton ever imagined.

For a long time this boldly patterned shorebird, slightly bigger than a pigeon, was almost extinct. The wealthy gunners of the nineteenth century, the clubmen of the Atlantic coastal resorts, some of whom killed thousands of shorebirds in a single day for sport, came close to destroying the willet. They succeeded in destroying the Eskimo curlew. Mass slaughter for sport ceased to be respectable just in time to save the willet, which in recent years has been slowly reoccupying its former range, and spreading northward through Nova Scotia. Today it nests all along the shores of Annapolis Basin, as it did in early Acadian times, each pair the tenants of a patch of salt marsh or of a clearing in the nearby woods. They feed on the mud flats, pulling marine worms from their burrows, and snapping up the so-called beach fleas, the *Orchestia*, which look more like tiny shrimps than fleas, and the larval flies that live by the millions under ropes of rotting seaweed cast up by the Fundy tides.

The willets nest in a little clearing in our ravine, as well as on the salt marsh near our beach, and often perch on our roof-tree, calling loudly to one another: 'Kiddily-dee! Kiddily-dee!' a call that they repeat as they circle overhead protesting human intrusion on their nesting territory. I have to stretch my imagination pretty far to imagine one of them calling 'Pill-will-willet,' as they are said to do along the American shores in migration. Perhaps they speak a different language in the south. They arrive here in April and immediately advertise their presence with conspicuous territorial flights and loud musical calls. Much more than the quiet robins (some of whom may be here all winter), the willets are the true criers of the spring.

Because I live in the middle of a colony of nesting willets, I have been privileged to see their courtship dance as Audubon and Bent never did. Indeed, up to the time Bent published his *Life Histories* no one had ever reported seeing this fanciful dance, surely one of the most remarkable among all the dances of wild creatures.

The willet is a striking bird, with wing stripes that flash like flags, white on black, all the more brilliant because it is seen most often against the sombre background of the sand flat or the salt marsh. The bird engages in frequent display, holding the wings straight up as it stands erect (somewhat in the pose of a gilded archangel by Giovanni) showing off its bold design like a costume in a pageant. Such displays are thought to be a part of courtship, and they may often be just that, the bird, at a distance, signalling: 'Look at me! See how beautiful I am!' But the display is not a part of the dance. Once the birds are close together they no longer need display. Their interest already aroused, they concentrate on the symmetry of the dance without distraction.

As for the display, there need not be another willet around to see it. A bird that wants to show off its fine feathers will display in front of just about anything. A willet will show off to a flock of sandpipers, or to its own reflection in a pool of water. A yellow-shafted flicker will sit on a branch and display the golden lining of its wings to a chickadee or a redpoll. The most extreme example of inappropriate display I ever saw was a peacock displaying to a sparrow. Obviously there are motives other than courtship at work here. They could be territorial, warning off poachers. They could be nationalistic, drawing the group together. Or they could be simple self-delight, the kind of unstudied posing you see in a child displaying for the camera. Fashion models are taught to do this in eye-catching clothes, but even ten-year-olds will do it instinctively; I've seen the same pose again and again in nude children facing the camera, hands locked behind the head, smiling with self-delight: 'Look at me! See how beautiful I am!'

Willets nest on the ground, either in dry patches of the salt marshes along our shore, or in the adjoining woodland glades. They usually hatch four chicks, which promptly leave the nest and follow their parents about, cheeping to be fed on worms, slugs, or insects from the beaches. The chicks are not often seen by casual visitors to the shore, for they are very secretive until ready to fly, and very inconspicuous in their mottled camouflage. In danger or alarm an adult will pick up a chick, and fly off to safety with the youngster clamped between its legs, returning for others until the whole brood is removed. By late summer, when fully fledged and grown, young willets become quite bold, flying in small flocks, often five to ten birds together, along the tide line, or wheeling overhead to inspect intruders walking through their favourite feeding ground.

In late summer or early autumn many small flocks of willets from other nesting colonies appear along our shore, fattening themselves for their overseas flight to the southern Atlantic coast or the West Indies. From my canoe around Goat Island or Porter's Point I have seen assembled flocks of perhaps a hundred and fifty of them at one time. They pass on southward to St. Mary's Bay, and finally depart from Cape St. Mary's, Yarmouth, or Cape Sable, flying perhaps a thousand miles over the ocean before they touch land again. My neighbour Bill Percy sees them on the Florida beaches in early spring, and I in March on the beaches of South Carolina, each of us wondering if they are the same birds we see at home.

How do they navigate? Apparently by the sun and the stars. They have a grid at the back of the eye that is supposed to act as a star chart, though nobody can explain exactly how it works; it isn't the kind of thing you can discover by cutting up a willet and looking at the scraps under a microscope. But though their flight is direct and true in clear weather, they become lost in fog. If the weather remains 'thick' for a long time they will collect in a flock, alight on the sea, and wait for the weather to clear. This seems to rule out magnetic navigation (suspected in some other birds) and to suggest that they orient themselves by the sky. Perhaps they cannot fly above the clouds, as some migrants can do, but they are well able to rest on the water like a flock of phalaropes, and, with semi-webbed feet, are fairly well equipped for swimming.

A hundred years ago many thousands of Eskimo curlews used to gather here, just as the willets gather today, feeding on the ripe berries and the burgeoning insect life of late summer, working southward until they reached the islands around Shelburne and Barrington Passage, where they began a flight of epic proportions; they would cross the open ocean in a great sweep of five thousand miles to South America and then fly over the jungles and the pampas to the high plateau of Patagonia at the distant tip of South America, returning through central Canada to the Arctic in the spring. In those days there may have been a hundred thousand curlews over Annapolis Basin at one time.

Gunners here and in Labrador found them an easy target. Like passenger pigeons, they were killed for market; the Hudson's Bay Company bought them and canned them for export. The teal-sized birds were so tame and easy to shoot that gunners quickly exterminated them. A favourite trick was to capture a wounded curlew and keep it alive as long as possible, making it scream its distress call. Instead of warning away its companions, as would happen with so many other birds, this attracted them. They came flying to the aid of the wounded bird, and were destroyed in their turn. The biggest slaughters of all took place in the American Midwest during the spring migration, when Eskimo curlews were hauled away by the cartload.

By 1900 the once-plentiful curlews had become rare. By 1910 they were no longer worth pursuing for meat, but had achieved great value as museum specimens. Then, as now, there were 'scientists' who believed that no bird had achieved its highest destiny until it was stuffed and labelled and stored in the drawer of a museum. So, as happened with other rare birds, skin-hunters exterminated the last Eskimo curlews in order to sell them to the taxonomists. The last birds ever certainly seen alive were shot in Argentina in 1924 and 1925 for a museum in Buenos Aires. There have been doubtful reports of survivors from time to time ever since.

The curlews always flew in mixed flocks with golden plovers, which were also hunted to what seemed like extinction. John James Audubon was with a party of gunners near New Orleans in March 1821 when they exterminated an estimated forty-eight thousand golden plovers in a single day. But a few golden plovers survived and increased when at last such massacres were outlawed. By the 1950s I was seeing golden plovers quite frequently on the Newfoundland tidal flats. By the 1980s they were still uncommon, but by no means rare during autumnal migration in Nova Scotia. I saw them on the rim of the basin in 1985 with mixed flocks of sandpipers and smaller plovers.

Meanwhile, that other curlew of the east, the Hudsonian, also a companion of the golden plover, seems to have survived fairly well. Unlike the similar Eskimo curlew, it is a wild bird, difficult to approach, found often on barrens far from tidal flats, feasting on blueberries and partridgeberries with its smaller companions until it is ready to leave on its flight across the ocean. This curlew still forms mixed flocks with golden plovers. No one has ever explained the symbiosis between curlews and plovers, but it must exist. Perhaps one species is a more efficient navigator, and the other a more efficient sentry. Something like that. For it is only during migration that the birds show this strange need for companionship between totally different species.

The dancing willets helped to reconcile me to an idea that I spent most of my lifetime rejecting – the fundamental place of dance in nature. I grew up in a world where human dancing was 'dry fucking,' a Hollywood perversion in a class with the

'French kiss,' and that may be why I rejected it out of hand. Neither Nietzsche nor Havelock Ellis, with their meditations on the dance, reconciled me to its fundamental nature, but nature herself eventually did. If shorebirds and chimpanzees and honey bees all dance, and if fundamental particles dance in the cloud chamber, who am I to deny the cosmic connection?

The mesons dance like a swarm of bees, living and dying in the flickering cloud. They appear like sparks and vanish, but, unlike sparks, dying they restore the balance, return their parent to the state she enjoyed before their birth. It is as though they might be a small burst of exuberance, a signal only, like the honking of geese, proclaiming the passage through eternity of a living body.

Rhythm begins far down in nature, perhaps as far down as the resonance of fundamental particles – which may, after all, be not quite so fundamental as once was supposed; it paces the universal dance of the molecules; it is inherent in the quartz crystals that keep our watches running on time. The earth dances with the sun and the moon, creating the regular rhythm of day and night, of summer and winter, of spring tide and neap tide. All those rhythms in turn are transmitted to living creatures: we see them most notably in the slow dance of the sea anemones in a tidal pool, in the rising and falling of the worms on a clam flat. Even in the darkness of a laboratory tank, shut away from the daylight and the outside world, such creatures will continue the rhythms that their ancestors learned on the shores of some vanished ocean, taught to them by the dance of the solar system, in the years when life was young.

Dance is rhythm in four dimensions: the three dimensions of space, and the fourth that we call time. It seems to be fundamental in the world. My children danced without ever being instructed, without even having a suggestion made to them. When the rhythms of music stirred them (as I played a mouth organ) they got out on the floor and began dancing.

Birds of many species dance – crows, partridge, herons –

some a grave minuet, others a wild tarantella. More mammals than hares dance in more months than March. I have seen a wolf dancing with his shadow, and have heard that even elephants, those eight-ton mammoths with legs like the trunks of trees, solemnly dance in their jungle glades, as well as in human circuses.

Rhythm may well be as fundamental in the universe as order. Just as we see the crystals of copper sulphate fashioning themselves into blue-green fronds like prophecies of trees billions of years before the first trees were imagined, so we see the particles in the meson cloud living out their lives in a perfectly regular dance at a level of organization so primitive that even matter, as we know it, does not yet exist, not to mention the life and the social orders and the flow of history that will emerge from this meson dance ten billion years later.

Order, pattern, symmetry, rhythm – all may seem to be abstract qualities, not to be considered in a class with matter and energy. And yet, when we think about the question, we may conclude that these abstract qualities could be just as fundamental to the universe as the 'forces' that bind the elemental particles into atoms, and are now pictured as still other particles with such fanciful names as 'gluons.' Order, pattern, symmetry, and rhythm operate at the highest and lowest levels of perception. The binary stars dance, and so do the Cepheid variables, those flashing stars that measure out the spaces between galaxies. The galaxies rotate about their cores, and perhaps even the galactic clusters, moved by the same principle as the mesons a million orders of magnitude away, move about one another in a pattern so slow that only the Ancient of Days could perceive it.

But the meson who lives only a few billionths of a second is also a partner in the divine dance. And the willet, who lives in the half-way house between the meson and the galaxy, dances before god like David the king, saying yea and amen to the great flow and rhythm of life.

8

Island in the Stream

As soon as Andrew was big enough to handle a small pair of oars he began paddling across Fool's Run in an inflatable boat, often with Leah as a passenger. They picked berries on Goat Island. They visited the gulls that inhabit its eastern shelf; they watched the great blue herons fishing along the edges of the tidal flats. The island (I wish it had a lovelier name – why couldn't it have been named for the gray seal or the white dolphin instead of for the domestic goat?) is a detached piece of Porter's Point, separated by deep channels from the land on either side. But it has great semi-submerged banks of sand and mud – banks that dry out at low tide, upstream and downstream, until the total area of its tidal flats is at least six or seven times larger than the area of the island itself.

The tides, though swift, are not much of a hazard, running at about two and a half knots, but rising impressively some twenty-five feet, or occasionally even higher, thus helping to isolate the island by creating a problem for heavy boats: beached, they could be half a mile from the water at low tide; anchored, they could be half a mile from shore at high tide. The first time I rounded the island in a boat I was startled to see what looked like a tide rip a quarter of a mile long stretching out toward Port Royal. It was a sandbar, with the ebb tide flowing over it.

At the children's urging I began visiting the island by canoe (inflatable boats not being my choice for travel by sea) and soon came to treasure the relative isolation I could find there. It was rather like a portion of the Annapolis Basin as it must have been when Lescarbot first saw it in 1606.

The island has a breeding colony of herring gulls – a noisy, boisterous community, screaming and squawking, with a lot of symbolic squabbling, and loud protests against intrusion. I once did a summer's work, under the direction of Dr. L. M. Tuck, in a colony of ring-billed gulls, but was never able to share Tinbergen's pleasure in close contact with such creatures. I prefer them well beyond arm's reach – which seems to be the way the gulls prefer me, too. Fortunately, there's a good deal of room on Goat Island. They can have their noisy and messy colony at the eastern end, so long as they leave the beaches for me, and a quiet bit of woodland for the songbirds and the varying hares.

The gulls' habit of nesting in colonies seems to be a useful defence against predators. They quarrel endlessly among themselves, and defend their tiny patches of nesting territory with noisy threats and occasional attacks. They will even kill stray chicks that come too close to their territory. But the squabbling neighbours will band together to mob a fox, will unite to attack a weasel or a mink, or perhaps even to drive off a hawk – anything of moderate size that seems to threaten them by daylight will be fought off. A few clever foxes have got around this defence by raiding gull colonies at night, when the birds are dopey with sleep. That may be why the gulls choose places like Goat Island. Foxes hate to swim, though they will do it well enough if pressed, and the swim across Fool's Run is hardly an inviting one. So the colony remains relatively free from predation.

Nowadays human visitors are not much of a bother, either. Fifty or a hundred years ago Goat Island was a popular summer resort. Quite a few people lived there temporarily in cabins, and bands of picnickers and berry-pickers visited it frequently. But the automobile has almost ended such visits. Anyone with a day to spare now is more likely to go off in a car than a boat. So Goat Island has been returned to the gulls and the wilderness.

Though this is hardly an area of 'free beaches,' Goat Island is a place where you can swim in the nude. On a hot August afternoon I silently rounded one of its headlands by canoe, and came unexpectedly upon a pair of nude swimmers. The woman modestly sank down to chin level in the water, while the man retreated behind a boulder, waiting for me to pass by, but I had no intention of landing and upsetting their solitude. I passed on, rounded another headland, and in the cove opposite Porter's Point, where there is a shingle beach, I came upon a group of young campers who looked as if they'd been going nude all summer, their bottoms as brown as walnuts. Completely unselfconscious, they all came running down to the water's edge, to welcome me ashore.

They had built for themselves a kind of primitive resort. Using flotsam collected from the sand flat, they had rigged up a swing between two trees. A huge wharf timber had floated in from god-knows-where to become a combined seat and picnic table. For sleeping they had a big old canvas tent, for transportation, a small flat-bottomed boat. A trail from their camp led back across a tiny bog to the cool depths of Goat Island's miniature forest, to the haunts of the hermit thrush, the sapsucker, and the veery. Five hundred years ago young Micmacs must have camped here just like this.

They reminded me of my own children during our first years here, running nude on the beach and in the meadow. Even plain children can look beautiful in the nude, and our children weren't plain; they were lovely in face and form. Ignited by the sun of high noon, their bodies glimmered like flames among the tall wildflowers. They stood, pillars of life against the dark water, their nakedness more eloquent than speech, more beautiful than the surrounding flowers. I find it hard to credit the ugliness of a culture that forces its children to go clothed on all occasions, denying their natural grace, denying the beauty of their animal nature, treating them as Barbie dolls to be dressed up in flounces and bows. This is one of the perversions of our culture, an inheritance from the death cult that swept right through the western world in the days of the Roman decadence.

Asians, Africans, Egyptians, Greeks – across the world and through the centuries nude children have been loved and admired by those who loved life. In Greece they were part of every public ceremony; they accompanied wedding processions bearing cakes and flowers and singing, they danced at 'gymnopaedic' festivals, they served the priests in the temples. The nude boy was the universal symbol of ceremonial joy, of fertility, of the beauty of life. It is one of the ironies of history that the altar boys of the Christian churches are the direct descendants of the naked young pagans who served the priests of Grecian temples at the rites appropriate to the titular gods of their cities.

In Christendom children had to be swaddled, preferably in thick layers of cloth that disguised their animal form, and helped to deny their animal nature. Even today, when we have rejected so much of the claptrap that the Christian Dark Ages passed down to us, our children are required to observe obscene clothing taboos: witness little girls in two-piece bathing suits. A few lucky children go nude as toddlers; then, at the age of five or so, they are plunged into school (if they haven't been plunged even earlier into *nursery* school), and the world closes around them. The change, the tarnishing, begins with that plunge into the barbarian culture with which the child of liberated parents is besieged, the death culture that descended upon us from Syria, the dying-god cults that infected the late Empire in the days of Hadrian and Marcus Aurelius, and spread like a blight over the brightness and beauty of the earth, denying man's animal nature and the joy of the world, and the light of the mind and the heart. Even for those who now reject the mystery cults, with their blood sacrifices, their emblems of torture, and their worship of death, the weight of the past remains; how few of those who have made their intellectual escape from the Judaeo-Christian traditions are able to come down from the cross, to open themselves to the engulfing tide of joy that is the true essence of the world!

I have a picture dating from the 1920s of a street in the city of Niamey on the upper Niger. It shows horsemen fantastically dressed in quilted armour, like knights of the First Crusade. In the background two boys, aged ten or eleven, are watching the show. One boy is black, and naked. The other is white, dressed in shoes and stockings and breeches, a shirt and a buttoned vest and a hat. Apart from the fact that the black boy looks beautiful and the white boy looks absurd, the picture speaks volumes about colonialism and culture clash, and the peculiar kind of prudery that allowed children with dark skins to run about city streets in the nude while their white-skinned friends could expose nothing below their chins.

It is one of the sad facts of life in Africa today that newly emergent societies are aping the silly, obsolete dress codes of the European and American colonialists. Upper-class and bourgeois Africans go around trussed up in suits and ties and black leather shoes, no matter that the temperature is 40^{0}c. in the shade! The light, often beautiful, tribal dress is discarded. And barefoot children aren't allowed in public libraries. The unwashed monks of the Dark Ages have cast a long shadow.

As the clouds pass over the great bay the flickering flames of the young campers on the Goat Island beach are eclipsed. Where they were living creatures of light, they have become mere wraiths, standing in the shadow. So with time they may be eclipsed in fact as well as in vision, but for me, now, they stand as doors of perception with the sapling and the unfolding flower, leading into the infinite.

Surrounded here by the upwelling of creation, seeing children run nude through the sunlight, seeing trees stretch upward in a single summer higher than I can reach, watching the moon spread the creeping ocean into the grass of my field, I know that all things are sacred and numinous, and living in a ferment of divine grace. And I think what a tragedy it is that so many of us have turned our backs on all this, striking out of the hand of the gods the bread and wine that they offer, to retreat into the ascetic tower of spiritual pride. For one who flees from the world into the barrenness of the spirit finds not god, but an idol; the world is the very flesh and blood of god, dancing with the heavenly fire. Those who attain truly to the love of god, love not god solely in her unity, but god also in her diversity: god in child and man and galaxy, god in moth and leaf and thorn. The world is god dancing, god beside himself.

Life, a process of becoming, holds transience at its very heart. The live flower that withers on the stem is far lovelier than the dead imitation, which may collect dust, but otherwise will not change. There are people who wish their children would never grow up – an understandable wish in a world where they will most likely be tarnished and corrupted and destroyed. It is indeed tempting to wish that the five-year-old in your arms or the ten-year-old eagerly helping you plant a tree could just remain that way forever. But in fact anything that doesn't change is a mere ornament; not a kitten, but a china cat, not a living rose, but a silken imitation. It is the fourth dimension, the dimension of change, that gives to living things a level of reality wholly beyond that of the loveliest artifact ever created. I have always been bothered by Yeats's ambition (expressed in 'Sailing to Byzantium') to get 'out of nature,' and to become 'such a form as Grecian goldsmiths make,' enjoying the spurious immortality of a clockwork bird singing from the limb of an artificial tree. It is true poetry, but the poetry of decadence, appropriate to Byzantium, not the poetry of life, where all things move and change and melt into other forms, and defy the Second Law of Thermodynamics by forever building grander and more intricate temples for the Holy Ghost. We know that Pygmalion could not really have fallen in love with the stone woman, Galatea. The story is a parable; the artist, too, can fall into the trap of spiritual pride, perhaps almost as easily as a bishop. But love is a tragic passion. We can love only things that are passing on toward death and apotheosis.

And though life is mortal, it is bound up, in ways that are difficult to understand or express, with an eternal reality. The mortality, the change, the flux through which the whole universe passes, is, in a sense, only the colour that plays over its surface. Underneath, there is an essence that remains diamond-like and immutable, difficult as that may be for us, who are part of the changing colour, to apprehend.

I recall the definition of beauty proposed by the mystical philosopher Plotinus: the translucence of the eternal splendour shining through the creation. I can think of no kind of beauty it fails to define. When I stand in the great trench running between the mountain ranges of western Alberta, and contemplate Mount Columbia, I have the same perception of the eternal order as when I look into the contours of a flower, or admire the supple body of a sun-browned child. Nor does it end with the creatures of the universe. The same beauty, the same translucence of eternal splendour, is found even in abstract things. The child's toes, lying in my hand, a beautiful set of harmonic curves, give me pleasure very similar to the pleasure I feel when contemplating the most abstract kind of symmetry – that, for example, which exists between the squares and the prime numbers.

I have never been quite sure whether the beauty of the abstract exists by itself or not. Perhaps the beauty that we see in harmonic series or in mirror symmetry is actually a projection from the human body, an echo, as it were, of pairs of breasts producing symmetrical parabolas, variations on the themes of hands and feet that are not only bi-symmetrical, but also serial within their symmetry. Which is to say that the translucence of eternal splendour may in reality be only our love for members of our own species projected into the universe at large. And I'm not at all sure that we'd find the decimal system such a perfect way of ordering numbers if we had flippers instead of hands, or only eight fingers instead of ten.

I tend to believe, however, that a system of feedback is at work here, a reinforcing loop. I believe that the translucence of the eternal splendour shining through the creation does, indeed, inform and reinforce the love I feel for the child I hold in my arms, or the woman I embrace in sexual union, and that this love in turn strengthens my perception of the eternal splendour in the gem-like globes of our solar system and the great wheels of the galaxies shining against the everlasting night.

9

The Basin
and the Stars

The true greatness of the fifth Brandenburg concerto does not consist in the dexterity with which its parts are interwoven and developed – all that is mere dress, presentation – the greatness consists in the sheer, inexpressible magic of the first theme. Everything else, including the famous harpsichord solo, is essentially the setting for this pure jewel of musical inspiration. J. S. Bach is often praised for the 'architectural' style of his music. All very well, except that he transcends architecture exactly the way that the Taj Mahal transcends it. Great ideas, great visions, great musical themes, all have this inexpressible spiritual quality that places them beyond analysis, beyond the reach of the critics, beyond any explanation that we can offer.

It is in nature as in art. The field naturalist working for the government, the ecologist working for the oil company, are well able to see the world's parts, and how they fit together, perhaps even to wax eloquent over the 'web of life' or the 'fragile ecosystem,' which are but the dressing, the presentation, the architecture. There are magic experiences in nature, as there are in music. Sitting alone in a canoe on a great bay on a windless evening as the tide begins to flow and the seals slip one by one from their ledges is such an experience, a spiritual awakening like listening to Bach or viewing the Tahitian canvasses of Gauguin or reading the thirty-sixth stanza of Shelley's *Adonais*. Experiencing this magic, this inner essence of the universe, wherever it may be found, is one of life's great fulfilments.

My canoe sits on the water like the seed of the willow herb floating on the air. Here the world is no longer flat; it is many-layered like a crystal. The red fronds of the seaweed reach upward toward the bottom of the boat, the round blue domes of the mussels climb the towers of the rocks, the coralline algae grow like the trees of some forest in a Celtic myth. There is no motion, no *sense* of motion, in the still canoe on the glasslike surface of the sea. But the sunken world with its living blanket of white and yellow and red goes streaming past, carried on a cosmic conveyor belt, moving off into the otherwhere of space-time.

This is the Fundy tide, the fingers of the moon, the space-warp that connects me to the regions between the planets, and in my green canoe on the colourless water I am as truly a space traveller as anyone orbiting the earth in a thick metal carapace – more truly, perhaps, since I am naked in the universe, slipping like a seed along the grooves of the solar whirlpool, not clanking along like a suit of Teutonic armour which may, in fact, have nothing but a skeleton inside; I am a living mote in its tide, part of the flow, a portion, however small, of the becoming.

The stars come out, gleaming against the night; Goat Island rises like a moated castle, black against the Fundy shore, and overhead the deeps expand into the everlasting night, into the whirlpool of our origins, out of which the sun and the earth emerged. Down in the depths of the basin I observe them, pale tides of photons flickering in the gloom, singing the yesterdays, speaking of the fathomless depths of time, of a flow so vast that my life within it is an all-but-invisible flicker, and the whole of human history no more than the blink of a cosmic eye. I know that some of those streams of photons have come to me across billions of years of time and space. The sky pours down upon me in endless streams connecting me to the most remote events in a universe where nothing that has ever happened ever ceases to happen.

The stars. Yes. As I float on the basin, seeing them above and below me, I have the sense of time-travelling in a universe of stars. And how much more wonderful they are than men dreamed they could be, even as recently as a century ago! My grandfather loved to sing a hymn with the lines:

> He made the stars, those heavenly flames,
> He counts their numbers, calls their names. . . .

That was what they seemed to be in my grandfather's time. Though they were known by then to be suns, not mere flickering lights, as they may have seemed in the time of *his* grandfather, they were still assumed to be mere bonfires in space. Only in the past few decades have we begun to appreciate the true nature of a star – its long and complex history, the marvellous processes that take place in and around it, the awesome chain of evolution by which it comes into being and through which it enriches the near and distant regions of its galaxy. A star, like a great poet, is a centre of creative energy, and leaves behind at its death great stores of wealth that did not exist before.

'A star's substance, totally indifferent to life,' Loren Eiseley pronounced. I profoundly disagree. Far from being indifferent to life, a star and a star's substance are pregnant with life's origins. A star is to life as a mother is to her children. Dylan Thomas's 'force that through the green fuse drives the flower' flows straight from the heart of a star. Life is a star's efflorescence, its bloom and its fruit, one of the means by which it projects itself outward through space-time into eternity.

Nineteenth-century thinkers, faced with a bald contradiction between the concept of a divine providence solicitous of every sparrow's fall, and what seemed to them to be ruthless massacre on every hand, often arrived at positions of despairing agnosticism. Tennyson saw nature as wasteful and cruel:

So careful of the type she seems,
So careless of the single life.

Had he looked further he might have seen the type also, what we call the species, destroyed almost as recklessly as the individual. For every living species, a thousand are extinct.

Emerson looked on the appalling destructiveness of natural forces, the infinite prodigality and wastefulness of suns and systems, and insisted there must be a universal, though non-human, goal toward which it moved. Today we see much further, though few of us believe in universal goals or ends, those relics of theology passed down to us from the deistic religions.

The prodigality and wastefulness that we see, for example, in the explosions of supernovae, the young, massive stars, are not wasteful at all, but an essential step in the vast structure of chemical evolution. The exploding star, which has 'cooked' the heavy elements in its heart, spreads this newly created substance through the galaxy, making possible second-generation and third-generation stars and planets rich in the elements that will evolve toward life.

By means of its explosion the supernova is spreading through space the seeds of birdsongs and symphonies, of spaceships and civilizations, and perhaps, at the same time, is providing the percussion, the trigger, which will start another round of physical evolution in neighbouring solar systems. Such is the current theory.

So, too, the millions of species that have vanished, that have gone before us and have become extinct, were not 'mistakes' subsequently wiped off the slate. They were essential parts of the evolving ecosystems in which they lived, a process to which there is no end, and no goal unless it is one of ever-increasing complexity and beauty, striving, if you like, toward infinite levels of being that will never be achieved.

The watching stars. I still wonder if they *do* watch. It is not impossible, not even, perhaps, unlikely. It could be that we are watched with amusement, with compassion, or even with hope. The coldness, the indifference, of the stars is almost a platitude. But are they indifferent? They do not speak to us, it is true. That may be because we have not yet learned to speak to *them*. To believe that we are unique, that we inhabit the only living world in the galaxy, is close to a total absurdity. On the contrary, as the astronomer and cosmologist Fred Hoyle pointed out in a convincing statistical argument, knowing what we now know about stellar and planetary evolution, we should expect earth-like planets to be the rule rather than the exception among stars of the main sequence, and we should expect life to develop on every such planet.

As I look into the dome of stars above the basin, or down into the still depths where they are reflected, I am convinced beyond argument that this galaxy is the domain of life throughout its extent, that thousands of the stars I see provide life's energies to thousands of living worlds, and that millions, *billions*, of others circle through the darkness beyond the range of my vision, providing the fuel of life for worlds that are indeed as numberless as the sands on the seashore; for the living planets in the universe are probably much more numerous than the grains of sand on the surface of the earth.

What kind of life shares the universe with us? All kinds that are possible. But we should remember that biology, even if it works by trial and error, does not lead to accidental results. It is a grave mistake to think of humans, for example, as the end result of a long series of random accidents. Quite the contrary. Biology, even if its mutations are accidental, tends to find the best, if not the only, solution to the problems of the environment. Consequently the adaptive forms that we see around us are not accidental, but very nearly inevitable.

This does not mean that life throughout the universe is uniform. A star slightly more or less luminous than our sun, or one with a slightly different colour spectrum, might produce a biology with patterns quite different from our own. But we should expect the *chemistry* of life to be basically uniform throughout, based upon the uniform chemistry of the inorganic and organic levels of chemical evolution that we observe in the stellar clouds and the interstellar spaces. And where conditions are similar (on 'earth-like' planets) we should expect similar life forms to evolve.

The native animals of Australia are an outstanding example of this principle at work. The marsupials managed to cross into the sixth continent before mammals had reached the adjoining parts of southeast Asia. The mammals did not arrive until humans (the so-called Aborigines) built seagoing boats. Meanwhile the environment of Australia produced from the marsupial stock a range of creatures that looked and acted remarkably like the mammals that evolved in other parts of the world. After millions of generations you had a marsupial 'mouse,' a marsupial 'rat,' a marsupial 'fox,' a marsupial 'raccoon,' a marsupial 'wolverine,' a marsupial 'cat,' a marsupial 'wolf,' even a marsupial 'tiger.'

There could be no more convincing demonstration that evolution follows inevitable routes. Even when it starts with quite different materials, it will produce, in similar environments, quite similar forms.

So it is no accident that we have raccoons prowling through our meadow at Annapolis Basin. I am quite convinced that if the moon were as big as the earth (and consequently had atmosphere, water, and life) there would be 'raccoons' there too.

Parallelism in evolution is not pushed to absolute limits. Its results are similar, not identical. The marsupial wolf looks like a wolf, acts like a wolf, but does not have the same metabolism, or quite the same organs of structure. Given time, the Australian fauna might have included marsupial apes, and even a bipedal marsupial hominid with an advanced culture. It would not be in the least unlikely.

On an alien planet of earth-like mass, orbiting a sun very similar to our own, I would expect to find plant and animal life, including forms similar to our mammals, but perhaps not true mammals at all, and quite certainly not able to interbreed with anything on this planet. I would expect that the eye, an inevitable organ that has developed separately in various terrestrial phyla, would have evolved on billions of other planets. I would expect that in many instances vision would have become binocular. I would expect that sex, invented separately by plants and animals on earth, would have been discovered in most of the places where plant-like and animal-like life exists. I feel sure that bird-like creatures fly through the air of remote planets. Some of them are probably 'woodpeckers,' and some of them 'hawks.'

But my primary interest lies not in such speculations. What concerns me is the way in which evolution, taking the elements of chance, of random mutations (if that is what they are), can produce from them a result that is not in the least haphazard, but that fits very closely into an inevitable pattern determined by the materials with which evolution has to work, modified by the environment in which it has to function. The Australian fauna and the Darwin finches of the Galapagos Islands are both outstanding examples of this. When a finch evolves into a woodpecker it is no accident.

The distinction between living and non-living matter is rather straightforward: living tissue is based on the nucleic acids; non-living tissue is not. However, it would be quite wrong to go on from there to an assumption of 'superiority' for living things, which are not necessarily of a higher order than some of the complex structures of non-living matter. A non-living star is an exceedingly complex organism, with a long and involved life history. The things that happen inside a star – the conversion of simple hydrogen atoms through long and complex chains of evolution into more and more sophisticated elements, some of them having intricate structures with hundreds of fundamental particles – are things that no living organism can duplicate, and are in their way quite as wonderful as the life history of a virus. The division of the universe into 'higher' and 'lower' orders of activity, with the higher orders assigned to life, is a simplistic, parochial judgment for which there is no justification. To assemble simple living organisms in the laboratory is a matter beyond our present skill, but by no means beyond the range of our possibilities. We cannot even imagine the powers we would need to synthesize a star.

The 'dead' chemicals of the universe arrange themselves in organized ways, in coherent and complex patterns, obeying a principle that is far older than life. Before the first living molecule had wrapped itself in a sheath of protein to form a primitive cell, water-borne gypsum was growing into stone flowers. I have gathered such flowers from the shore of the Annapolis Basin, and seen in museums even more striking examples. Before the first diatom had built its first glass house, quartz was growing to prismatic crystal towers, copper salts were forming fronds like ferns, and barite was fashioning what Charles Fort called 'the first rough sketch of a rose.'

The intricate patterns of the snowflakes follow directly from the structure of the water molecules, and this in turn follows from the nature of the bonds that hold them together. The shimmering point in space that we call an electron, the point where infinity meets the infinitesimal and creates a resonance that we can perceive, holds already within it the logic of the snowflake in its perfection and its infinite variety.

Matter is forever being ground down into amorphous dust and earth, and is forever rebuilding itself into the beautiful lattices of crystalline order, denying, even before life appears, that the universe is decaying into a heat sink or collapsing into a black hole. Rather, the principles of organization, of complex geometrical harmony, of all the forms of symmetry, are inherent in the most primitive levels of chemical evolution, and are certainly as much a part of the basic stuff of our universe as are the particles and waves and electro-magnetic fields that underlie everything we see and know and apprehend.

Life, and especially its non-material aspect, mind, is such an enormous force in the universe that we still have no concept of its ultimate significance. It wouldn't surprise me in the least to discover that this is what the universe is all 'about.' I suspect, without having a shred of proof, that life transcends the birth and death of the stars, and that mind may well outlast the final collapse of the universe, may, indeed, 'put on immortality.'

I do know this: mind is not an epiphenomenon. It is inherent in matter from the beginning, as essential a part of it as the 'forces' that bind the atoms. I cannot, of course, imagine what happens when a solar system becomes conscious, self-reflective, as ours is now in the very early stages of becoming; I can only speculate that it is as far beyond our imagining as television transmissions from the planet Uranus would have been beyond the imagining of Francis Bacon.

A solar system is but a speck, the equivalent of a single cell in the great body of the galaxy. What happens when a galaxy becomes conscious, self-reflective? But a galaxy is little more than a speck, the equivalent of a single cell in the great body of the universe. . . .

In his preface to *God and the New Physics* Paul Davies lists a number of 'deep questions': What is matter? What is life? What is mind? – questions that have been posed since humans began to think reflectively. Then he adds that we may be on the verge of answering them.

I do not agree. Nineteenth-century scientists thought they had answered those questions, but they hadn't. We may think we have answered them, after a fashion, by redefining them or embedding them in broader concepts. In this limited sense, we have already answered some of them. We know that life is chemistry. We know that matter can be reduced to energy waves. We know that mind depends on chemical and electrical processes in the brain. But in the fundamental sense the answers are as far away as ever. As we gain deeper understanding, deeper questions arise. If the Thing Beyond the Universe is infinite, as I strongly suspect it must be, we will never reach final answers to such fundamental questions. Infinity is not within the understanding of finite creatures; the deeper we probe, the more mysterious it becomes. So our physics today is in a far more complex state, far further from what looks like final answers, than it seemed to be in the time of Newton.

Dante, in his day, could discern a certain structure in the universe, a local, primitive structure centred about the earth or the sun. Newton, four hundred years later, observed it on a wider scale, extending a few million leagues beyond the earth to the 'fixed stars.' Today we see structures of incredible beauty reaching downward through orders of magnitude, one within the other like an infinite series of Chinese boxes, to levels far beyond those that the human imagination can grasp. And we see equally beautiful structures reaching upward through solar systems and star clusters and galaxies to levels equally beyond the imagination. I doubt that the human imagination can encompass even a single galaxy, a community of stars that may have more inhabited solar systems than there are human dwellings upon the earth. But a galaxy is a mere atom in the structure of the universe. It has form and beauty and ordered motion, its stars flowing about its centre in a perfect dance on a scale we cannot conceive. It is, though, only one of a great company in the galactic cluster, a community of galaxies following orders of structure and motion that we do not yet understand. And the clusters in turn are members of a community stretching outward through tens of billions of light years, all of them, perhaps, obeying laws of structure and motion beyond the wildest dreaming of cosmology.

There may be no such thing as chaos in the universe, only developing levels of cosmos, and no such thing as random motion, only portions of the universal dance that we do not understand. It is no idle matter to say that we shall never understand the whole, for every level of understanding that we have achieved, every magnitude of structure that we have discerned, has presented us with levels above and below until we might feel justified in speculating that the series of Chinese boxes is indeed infinite in both directions.

Infinite or not, the world that we know, the 'middle-sized' world that includes everything from microbes to stars, is a coherent structure tied together by a single principle, the principle of chemical evolution, the principle that, once you have even a hydrogen atom, all the rest must follow, and will continue so far as replication and increasing chemical complexity are possible.

Once chemical evolution has started, it will not stop unless it meets conditions that make further evolution impossible: such conditions as the 'brick wall' of great heat or great cold. Inside a star it can reach only the elemental level. Hydrogen will be cycled through deuterium to become helium. If the star is large enough, generating enough heat and pressure, the helium will be recycled further until it becomes carbon, oxygen, nitrogen – the basic elements needed for proteins – and on up the scale all the way to uranium and beyond. But here chemical evolution meets the brick wall of great heat. It can go no further. The same elements spewed into the corona of a star and into nearby space will cool until they begin to form compounds, and then organic compounds, which may drift away on the stellar wind and circulate through the galaxy for billions of years. They will evolve no further because they come up against the wall of extreme cold. But when such organic chemicals collect on the surface of a planet in the presence of appropriate gasses and liquids, with a star at the right distance, they will continue to evolve into the most complex chemicals of all, chemicals that can organize themselves into living creatures, and produce birdsong and chess games and spaceships. How much further than that evolution can go, we really have no idea as yet, but it may well be to levels that even Pierre Teilhard de Chardin could not have imagined. If the Thing Beyond the Universe is in fact infinite, then the evolution of the universe never has to stop. Not ever.

So as I float between the black deeps and the purple sky I see a living, palpitating universe, filled not with the clockworks of Kepler and Newton, but with the numberless company of immortals visioned by Blake. The world outpaces our imagination, and I can well believe that the universe I envision will seem to my grandchildren as naïve as my grandfather's 'heavenly flames' now seem to me.

My father, who saw the first horseless carriage drive along the dirt tracks of Newfoundland roads, could not have guessed in his wildest imaginings that he would live to see men scoop soil from the surface of Mars and send their cameras probing through the rings of Saturn and Uranus. No need to go back to my father's youth, or even my own. Eiseley, in his essay 'The Hidden Teacher,' recalls an encounter back in his student days with one of those whiz kids who could solve complex mathematical problems in seconds, then goes on to speculate that such living computers might be 'a new type of humanity,' representatives of the next evolutionary step, when humans might grasp the 'intangible web of the universe in all its shimmering mathematical perfection.' Eiseley wrote this in the 1960s and here, a mere fraction of a lifetime later, it has all gone for nothing. It is no longer possible to imagine that a human calculating machine might be 'the creature whose genotype could replace me.' Armed with a tiny calculator half the weight and thickness of a pack of cards, a calculator able to run forever on the power of mere daylight, even I can now outperform the boy wonder. His gift for computation now has about the same human-survival value as a set of antlers.

The world outpaces our imagination. But not our vision. The quality of vision brought to bear upon the world interprets its inner essence in ways that will not become obsolete like the models of cosmology. The universe that Newton imagined has passed away. The universe that Blake saw when he looked into the sky is as fresh as the day he reported it, for he saw behind the world of forms and appearances to the inner nature of things, the eternal core of reality.

10

Denizens of
Earth and Sky

It is the first day of July, and a flight of young willets, nineteen of them, comes wheeling over our beach. They are just recently fledged, but already can fly with skill and grace. Two adults, acting as guards for the whole flock, scream imprecations, making a great show of trying to drive me away. The noise soon brings three other adult willets from the nearby tidal flat to join the demonstration. It's quite an effective defence. Nobody would want to stay and listen to all that squawking.

We have a few thousand shorebirds living on the Fundy coastline in midsummer: willets, woodcock, spotted sandpipers. You have to go a bit further afield to find snipe. All the others nest either in the far north or in wilder parts of the country. By late summer there are literally millions of migrants visiting our tidal flats on their way between nesting and wintering grounds.

Semipalmated sandpipers arrive from the far north near the end of July. They are 'semipalmated' because of their half-webbed feet, not used much for swimming, but useful for running over soft mud or quicksand. These six-inch shorebirds nest near the northern tip of Labrador, around Hudson Bay, and along the arctic shore. They come here to fatten themselves on mud shrimp, of which we have vast numbers, before heading off past Brier Island or Cape Sable for the coast of South America, a flight of 2500 miles, sometimes made non-stop. An ounce or two of fat provides all the fuel needed for this incredible journey, and leads me to wonder whether body fat may not be the most efficient form of energy storage ever invented.

The shellfish that attracts the sandpipers is a European immigrant, a species of mud shrimp called *Corophium volutator* (it has no common name). Found only on the tidal flats of western Europe and the Bay of Fundy, it was doubtless introduced here accidentally by the same Acadian farmers who introduced the French willow to the Fundy salt marshes, and dyked and drained those marshes for pasture, hayland, and grain crops. This common little shellfish, only a fraction of an inch long, just the right mouthful for the sandpiper, may well have displaced similar native species that still occur on our tidal flats but are now relatively uncommon. It is doubtful, though, that they were ever as plentiful as this one. The tiny crustacean lives in a mud burrow whose walls it strengthens by a sort of glue that it secretes. It is equipped with paddles for flushing food-laden water through its burrow, and these burrows lie as thick as grass in a meadow. Other species of mud shrimp inhabit tidal flats from Labrador to Florida, but rarely in such abundance. You can dig *tens of thousands* of the Fundy mud shrimp from a single square metre of ground between high and low tide.

The clam flats – as we usually call them – are a great living nursery for plants and animals, for they enjoy the combination of abundant sunshine, at low tide, and abundant nutrients washed down in the rivers and brooks. Masses of seaweed clinging to scattered boulders are the most obvious sign of this burgeoning life, but the billions upon billions of microscopic diatoms that form a greenish scum all over the surface of the mud are even more important as the basis of the food chain. These single-celled plants, so small that ten thousand could sit on your thumbnail, have learned how to do something that no larger plant can manage. They build their own solar green-houses, enclosing themselves in iridescent shells of prismatic glass that traps sunlight and converts it to heat and growth. I have wondered whether those highly ornamented shells of glass might also act as a sort of solar filter, favouring the wavelengths of sunlight most useful to the growth of diatoms, and screening out the less useful ones. I can easily imagine the design of an experiment to test this, but, being too lazy for research, I have never followed up the idea.

In any case, they proliferate in the sunlight between tides, and provide food for many small species of shellfish which live on or just under the surface, and are often equipped with little built-in vacuum-cleaners especially adapted for sucking up diatomaceous ooze. Such minute grazing animals! Larger, carnivorous invertebrates eat them, of course. So do some small fish and birds. Each species is the food factory for something larger, till you arrive at the eagles, the herons, and the seals.

The milky ribbon worms are among the commonest large animals of our tidal flat. They are fragile. You have to dig carefully to get one out of the mud without breaking it. Their common name describes them well. They are wide and flat and run to a metre, or even more, in length. But ours are pink, rather than milky, except in the breeding season, when the males turn bright red, and the females a sort of reddish-brown. They inhabit long burrows in the mud, about one to each square metre, which would give us a population of perhaps fifteen million in Annapolis Basin. Needless to say, they are choice prey for the larger animals.

Soft-shelled clams, very abundant here, are among the favourite meals of gulls, ducks, and humans. Gulls and ducks in turn are taken by the largest hawks, including the rare bald eagles that we see from time to time cruising at tree-top height along the shoreline. The eagle is a long way removed from the diatom in its tiny glass shell, but it is the diatom that converts sunlight to life and makes many higher forms of life possible.

The mud flats are not the only food-producers in the basin.

The bloom of the plankton in the surface water also depends on nutrients washed down into the bay by the numerous rivers, small and great: the mighty St. John, the modest Annapolis, the tiny Ryerson Brook, each contributing its share. Billions of minute copepods swarm at the surface, feeding on the algae, and these little shellfish, very rich in oil, in turn feed mackerel, herring, alewives, and shad, all of which provide food for humans, as well as for ospreys, eagles, and the larger fish.

The seaweeds, too, are a basic food resource. In spring the Annapolis supermarkets sometimes offer 'marsh greens' for salads. Salty little green seaweeds, with hollow stems jointed like bamboo, they grow in pools between the clumps of grasses on the salt marsh. Many people also enjoy dulse, collected here by the ton, and usually dried for snack food, though it is also good for flavouring soup and stew and certain stir-fried dishes. It is an excellent source of protein, and has a full range of trace elements, including such exotic ones as molybdenum and gold.

The rockweeds (sometimes called 'bladder wrack') provide our land with most of the fertilizer it needs. The strands are shed from the rocks and drive up on the beaches in autumn. We collect it by the ton and haul it with our little tractor, to be washed by the rain and then incorporated into our gardens. The seaweed grows more vegetables than we can eat, and helps to fill our land with flowers, shrubs, and fruit trees.

The seaweeds are, of course, sunlight converters, but in addition they have mastered the trick of fixing atmospheric nitrogen. When they shed their strands, as they do once each year, and the strands wash up on the beach, they begin to decompose and to release the nutrients contained in their proteins. They decompose more readily than most land plants because they do not have the hard, woody cell structure that the land plants must build into themselves in order to remain upright in the air. The seaweeds are held upright by the water. So they start to release the nutrients from their soft cells almost as soon as they arrive on the beach.

Two classes of animals make immediate use of this abundant

food. One is the arctic seaweed fly, which is able to remain active all winter in our region, taking to the air whenever daytime temperatures rise above freezing, and hiding in the piles of rotting weed at night and on cold days. The other is the little shrimp-like creature commonly miscalled a beach flea, though it is not an insect at all, but an amphipod, a species of *Orchestia* shellfish that lives at the high-tide line or just above it. Every forkful of dead seaweed that I pick up is jumping with these lively creatures, and I feel a twinge of guilt at destroying them in such numbers, but of course the feeling is actually nonsense.

The beach fleas and the seaweed flies feed one of the loveliest of all shorebirds, the gorgeously coloured ruddy turnstone that arrives on our beaches at the end of July or early in August, still wearing its summer coat of black, white, and russet brown. The nearly robin-sized turnstones not only turn stones with their beaks looking for insects and worms; they also dig deep holes in the sand to capture snails, and root among the seaweed, snapping up the beach fleas. When they have fattened themselves sufficiently on this rich diet of shellfish, they will fly off to the Gulf of Mexico with their friends the black-bellied plovers. The word 'friends' is not out of place here. So close is the association between those two species of birds that hunters, in an era now happily ended, used to lure turnstones within gun range by imitating the calls of the plovers.

The turnstone is only transiently beautiful. By the time it leaves for its winter hunting ground it will have shed its gorgeous summer feathers for a coat of drab brown and gray, a camouflage that may have offered it some slight protection on the gun-haunted beaches of the south.

Ruddy turnstones are among the very few birds that you might see on all six continents (but not, except as a stray, in Antarctica). They have truly taken the world for their homeland. They nest as close to the north pole as they can get without actually laying their eggs on the sea ice. They spend their summers in Siberia, Alaska, Spitzbergen, and northern

Norway, but above all they seem to prefer the coasts of Greenland, Ellesmere Island, and the New Siberian Islands of the Soviet Arctic. Then they migrate to remote southern lands: Hawaii, Japan, New Zealand, Australia, South Africa, the Caribbean, Mexico, and the tropical islands of the Pacific. No one bird wanders all over the world. Those from Alaska head for the Pacific islands. Those from Siberia go to Australia or South Africa. Those from the eastern Canadian Arctic pass through Nova Scotia on their way to Jamaica and Mexico. Most of those migrations are of epic length – imagine flying from Alaska to New Zealand without gyrocompass or direction-finder!

How do they do it? No one really knows. Some hints of the mysteries behind bird migration have come to light in recent years, but much of it remains as great a mystery as ever, and in a way I'm not sorry for this. I once thought it important that we should know such things. Now it rather pleases me to discover that many of the so-called lower creatures possess senses far more subtle than our own, and powers that human arrogance cannot explain. I have read a lot of literature on bird migration, describing experiments and observations that the researchers hoped would explain the phenomenon, and I conclude that the researchers have barely touched the edges of the subject. Birds, like quarks, are beyond our present understanding. But then, we should remember that they may be a later product of evolution than the mammals, endowed with some of the tricks that nature only thought up after we had already been pushed out of her nest.

The tides sweep over the clam flats in a great flood twice daily. The migrants sweep through the sky in great flocks twice a year. These vast rhythms, so visible in such a small place, seem very like the heartbeat and the breathing of a living planet, interconnected as they are with each other, and with the manifold systems by which all other parts of the biosphere live and function and work together. The sun and moon, the winds and tides, the flowing rivers, the plants and animals, are all parts of a single whole, a marvellous unity that begins in the heart of the sun, and encompasses the orbit of the earth and the moon. It is the sun, as much as the earth, that puts forth flowers, the moon, as much as the salt marsh, that feeds the flocks of shorebirds.

It cannot be divided and separated and reduced to its parts. The exploratory surgery of the reductionist always kills the patient. When we try to explain great interlocking systems by dividing them, piece by piece, and subdividing the pieces, we create what Blake described as the 'death' imposed by the clockwork system of Newton. We touch not the hand of god, but the hand of Urizen, Blake's Spirit of Destruction. What we see is not the miracle of the creation, but its dead parts, its carcass rather than its living body and soul.

It is the living body and soul that I invite you to see.

In our time science has begun to have a human face. In the time of William Blake its face was monstrous, diabolical. Newton, in Blake's view, was an agent of death and sterility. Though he failed to realize it himself, Newton's clockwork universe was a denial of all living values, of spirit, of mystery, of god. Newton spent more time looking for god than he did looking for the springs that powered his mechanical universe, and it never occurred to him that the springs might be springs of inspiration. He never knew what it was he sought: some kind of omniscient clockmaker.

Blake understood this perfectly, and set himself diametrically against it. For him the universe was no clockwork, no machine, be it never so perfect, but the leaping fire of the creative imagination. For two centuries the clockwork model seemed to triumph, before it began to falter and run down. Maybe, the philosophers of science admitted, god had wound it up, back then, but everything since had followed in a pattern of precise mechanistic determinism. Such a view began to change only in the days of Einstein and Bohr. Now, a generation after them, we are able to make truly crucial discoveries: the discovery, for example, that a gorilla wants a kitten for a pet, and can learn to ask for it in a human language. Such an event could not have happened in the laboratories of Newton or Darwin. It could happen only in our time, when we have become sufficiently human to believe it possible.

We owe some of this change to people on the frontiers of theoretical physics – people who discovered that the objective world, the perfect clockwork of nineteenth-century science, was an illusion, that the universe is not so much a machine as an enigma wrapped in will and idea. We have also to thank the philosophical naturalists, men like Loren Eiseley and women like Sally Carrighar, who simply refused to accept mechanism, insisting that the whales are our brothers and the wolves our sisters. Newton made much of his humility before god, and his admirers have made much of his statement about playing with pebbles on the shore, but to listen to a gorilla asking for a kitten takes far more humility than Newton ever knew.

Humility before the beauty, the tragedy, the spiritual wonder of the universe around us, is indeed a rare quality. Not only the great mathematicians of the past, but even the great naturalists, who spent most of their time fitting the world into the neat little pigeonholes they had created for it, seem to me to have lacked such humility. I have seen it born, or reborn, during my own lifetime, in scientists such as Loren Eiseley and Fritjof Capra, in philosophers such as Lewis Thomas and Teilhard de Chardin, and above all in a host of common people who *care* about the world, not for some selfish reason, not just because they must live in it, but because it is infinitely worth caring about.

I pick up a small bird, dead from one of life's accidents. It has struck a power line – the power line, in fact, that I need in order to write this book. I hold it in my hand, a female Wilson's warbler, a jewel in green and gold, beautiful as a flower in death.

God sees the sparrow fall, but, as someone has observed, it falls anyway. Silly and limiting to think of god as a sentimental do-gooder. Such a view of nature, of the universe, limits only the viewer. Still, the death of the warbler fills me with regret for this fragment of lost beauty, for the nestlings who will not be fed, for the living world just a little poorer, at least for the moment. I have the right to be human, to hold this human viewpoint, to impart it to my children.

The universe is beauty and symmetry, order and complexity and chaos, the emergence of spirit from a mere turbulence of energy: good and evil have nothing whatever to do with this. They are peculiar to the narrow human limits. The 'problem of evil' exists on the social level. It looms large in the fairy tale and the nursery rhyme, in religious myth and social thought. Like the problem of poverty or the problem of urban blight it is real enough in the sphere of human relationships, but a matter of little consequence in the massive architecture of eternity. So the sparrow, or the warbler, falls, and only such humble creatures as I can be expected to care.

My son Andrew, aged eleven, wades out into the sea to rescue a struggling beetle thoughtlessly tossed into the water by another boy, a friend of ours. 'Leah and I rescue things,' he says. He holds the creature in his hand while the sun strikes dark-green fire from its carapace. 'How beautiful it is,' he adds, and carries it to a patch of grass where he hopes it will feel at home. It is not a question of being sentimental about insects. It is not 'reverence for life'; he knows well enough that the biting tick which he tears to pieces without a qualm is just as much 'life' as the beetle. What he admires, what he rescues, is life's magic, its beauty, its supernal manifestation in a creature as lovely as anything fashioned out of enamelled gold.

And it is that, the living body and soul of the universe, that I invite you to see.

11

Reptiles, Amphibians, and Evolution

Garter snakes, green snakes, red-bellied snakes, ribbon snakes, even big, beautiful constrictors: I never expected to live with so many handsome serpents around my feet.

I grew up with no fear of snakes, perhaps because none of my ancestors for ten generations or more had lived in a land where snakes could be seen. Some of them had come from Europe back in the seventeenth century, and must have known about vipers, but three hundred years of living in a land without snakes had wiped out the memory, and even the tradition.

My children, who also have no fear of snakes, have been handling them from infancy. Some of their first live pets were snakes. They weren't allowed to keep them very long, but it does a snake no harm to spend a few days fasting in a pottery bowl, or to be picked up and admired, so long as it returns to its natural haunts reasonably soon. It's a fact, though, that two of them escaped from a bowl on our living-room table and disappeared. Corky was quite upset at having snakes loose around the house, but nine or ten days later, when they got hungry and began to feel the urge to hunt, she found them slithering across one of our stone floors, and chased them outdoors with a broom.

Our first acquaintances among reptiles were garter snakes.

Fairly large, active by day, they are easy to see, and not too difficult to catch. Our meadow was a reasonably good place for snakes when we arrived, but the ravine, after we began restoring it with a stream and a series of ponds, became even better. The shady banks of a pond stocked with lots of frogs is the garter snake's ideal hunting ground. Most of ours seemed to be no more than a foot and a half long, but after the frogs became really plentiful we occasionally saw the grandfather of all the garter snakes, a creature that must have been four feet in length, stalking frogs around the shores of our lily pond. We sometimes found a nest of young, and discovered quite a range of colours in this single species. Besides the usual black and green and yellow, there was a rare checker-board pattern in pale gray and dark green. I actually had to look this one up in a snake book to convince myself that it was a garter snake at all. We've also seen them in soft brown and chestnut red. All very confusing.

Garter snakes, big and small, are really quite pleasant creatures to handle, docile and unaggressive (though I've seen one successfully fending off a pheasant by coiling and hissing and pretending to be a viper). If the weather is cool, they are grateful for human body warmth; a small one made a habit of crawling into my pocket and quietly coiling up there, presumably going to sleep. They have gleaming polished scales like bright enamel, cool and pleasant to touch, and they keep sniffing you with their flickering forked tongues.

Garter snakes hunt many things besides frogs. The smaller ones must live mainly on slugs, snails, and insects, which makes them very desirable things to have around a garden. Along with birds, toads, and predatory insects, the snakes have been successful defenders of our crops, so we've never needed even 'organic' pesticides, much less the violent poisons offered in the gardening shops and nurseries.

Two years after we began living here a major disaster overtook the garter snakes. The soil around Annapolis Basin rarely freezes much more than a foot deep in winter, and the snakes don't go very deep to hibernate. If they can find a large boulder and crawl under the middle of it, they hardly bother to get down into the ground at all; the mass of rock will provide enough heat storage to keep their bodies above the temperature of killing frost.

But we had a freak year. No snow came. None at all. The temperature dropped in December to -10^{0}c, then in January to -15^{0}c, and there were five to fifteen degrees of frost for weeks on end. With no snow to insulate the ground the frost line went down to two feet, perhaps to two and a half, and most of the garter snakes who had crawled confidently into their shallow dens for the winter never came out again. Only those who had gone deeper than their fellows, or had nested against the foundation of the house, or under a pile of rotting sods, or the like, woke up in the spring. For most creatures hiberation is a gamble of this kind, but one in which they have no choice: if they didn't take a chance on hibernation, they wouldn't be able to survive in northern countries at all. The garter snakes have since been recovering slowly, but they are still not as plentiful as they were before the great freeze.

We found our first red-bellied snake under a large flat stone near the house. The children brought it indoors, where it sat on my hand flicking its tiny forked tongue, like a flame in the mouth of a microscopic dragon. When you find your first red-bellied snake you're likely to think that it's a baby, just hatched. Ours seem to be no more than eight or ten inches long, and no thicker than a pencil. They are a rich, dark brown, velvety-looking, with belly scales of brilliant coral – quite charming, beautiful miniatures. One of my friends kept a live red-bellied snake on a fine gold chain with a tiny gold ring for a collar, and wore it as costume jewellery.

This little snake is also a valuable insect-hunter, thriving in organic gardens, but like many insect-eating birds it can be killed by pesticides – not on contact with the spray, perhaps, but by eating poisoned insects. It is also an active consumer of slugs, and of the eggs of slugs and beetles. You might think it too small to swallow anything as big as a slug, but like other snakes it can unhinge its jaws and swallow things much thicker than itself.

Andrew caught our first green snake, brought it indoors for everyone to see, and later released it into the garden. It was not much bigger than the red-bellied snakes, and also very beautiful, its scales on back and sides a brilliant green, its belly scales a dark ivory. This snake, too, is an insect-hunter, feeding mainly on caterpillars, and though it is sometimes called a grass snake, it often climbs up into blackberry canes and currant bushes, hunting its favourite food, the leaf-eating grubs.

Ribbon snakes are slender, wilder, and a good deal shyer than the garter snakes, very dark, with bright-yellow stripes along the sides. We see them most often in our cranberry bog, or among the pink fringed orchids in the wetter part of the meadow. They hunt small frogs and toads and mice, and also eat the eggs of song sparrows and bobolinks, if they happen to find them.

One bright summer day in 1985 Andrew came bounding into the house with news of an exciting discovery – a big, mottled snake that he had seen on our driveway, escaping into the shrubbery of the ravine. Big? Well, not quite as thick as his wrist, but long, and heavily blotched with olive green, bordered with black, on a white background.

This sounded so unlikely to me that I had him draw a picture of it. Then I looked it up, and sure enough, the drawing was an accurate representation of the pattern of the back and sides of a milk snake, a creature familiar in southern Ontario and in the middle Atlantic states, but, according to the range maps, found northward only to New Jersey on the coast. None were supposed to live anywhere in the Atlantic provinces, so far as I could learn. Well, this snake has obviously extended its range by many hundreds of miles since the books were written. Not only do we have it at Annapolis Basin, but Dr. Roseann Runte, president of the Université Sainte Anne, assures me that she has seen it at Church Point, thirty-five miles southwest of where we live. This suggests that it may now be established throughout southern Nova Scotia. How did it get here? It didn't swim across the Gulf of Maine, and it isn't likely that it migrated all the way from New Jersey to Northumberland Strait, then southward again for hundreds of miles to southern Nova Scotia. I'd guess that it hitch-hiked aboard transport trucks, in bales of hay or something of the kind, and crossed the Bay of Fundy on a ferry.

Anyway, it's a welcome immigrant. The milk snake hunts mostly at night, so you don't often see it. Its specialty is hunting mice and rats, which together provide seventy per cent of its food. It raids the nests of its prey, gobbling up the newborn young. Consequently it's a useful snake to have in a barn, a granary, or a feed mill. The snake's narrow head and slender profile are advantages for hunting rodents: anywhere a rat can go, a milk snake can follow; then it kills the rat by crushing it in its coils. I believe it is the only constrictor in Atlantic Canada.

Poisonous snakes are a real danger to humans, and give good grounds for worry because they are often invisible, or nearly so. You can look straight at a rattlesnake and fail to see it, its colours so closely match the rocks and the forest litter where the various species of rattlers live. But this worry ought to be banished from parts of the country where all the snakes are harmless.

Unfortunately the fear of poisonous snakes is often expressed as a hatred of all snakes, even in places where no poisonous snake has ever been found. I have seen a gang of young boys with sticks killing garter snakes in a field. Admittedly it was in Ontario, a more barbarous part of the country than this, but there may be places where it could happen here, too, and with the approval of the boys' parents. Snake hatred is so widespread that I suspect it may even be genetically transmitted. Needless to say, no snake in Nova Scotia is capable of harming humans, or of doing any damage to our interests. They are among the gardener's best friends. Wise gardeners should encourage and protect them by providing wild cover close to vegetable plots and flower beds, as we have done, leaving large patches of undisturbed land close to all our gardens, especially to provide cover for 'the creatures' – snakes, toads, shrews, and the like. It was one of the most useful things we did with any of our fifteen acres. I would urge all gardeners, if they have the space, to surround their cultivated land with undisturbed weed patches. Nothing else will give a garden such effective protection.

The amphibians tend to be less visible than the reptiles, but there are many to be found if you hunt for them. The only ones we see frequently are the green frogs that sit on the banks of the ponds, sunning themselves, so tame they will hardly bother to get out of your way. Indeed, if I move slowly and unaggressively I can slide a hand under them and lift them up. There are dozens – more like hundreds – of spring peepers, but getting a look at one of them isn't easy. The toads and the small forest frogs are also hard to see, each being well camouflaged against its background, but the beautiful little golden forest frog is well worth seeking out, as it crouches among the fallen leaves looking like a small splash of sunlight.

The temporary guests in our house included three species of amphibians: a red eft, a red-backed salamander, and a much larger spotted salamander, which is a lizard-like creature coloured almost black with bright-yellow polkadots. The spotted salamander spent a few days in a bowl with rocks and a little water before we released it to find a den in which to spend the winter. It vanished under one of our largest boulders.

Corky found the red eft sitting on our doorstep, apparently lost, for it clearly belonged in the woods. The eft is the 'land phase' of the common newt – a phase that lasts a surprisingly long time. It is born in the water, and has gills, like a tadpole, but it loses its gills, leaves the water, and becomes an air-breathing animal. It now looks like a miniature lizard with a small pointed snout, tiny feet and toes, and dark-red spots on an orange-red ground. An eft will walk around on your hand, quite unafraid. The even smaller red-backed salamander will do the same thing. Indeed, most small amphibians share this characteristic. They don't seem to object to being handled, so long as you do it gently.

The red eft spends two or three years in the woods, living in the moist litter of the forest floor, growing very slowly, and hibernating in winter in a natural hole under the roots of an old tree. One fine spring day the eft begins to change colour, and to lengthen out into a newt. It then returns to the water, camouflaged in brownish-green, and spends the rest of its life in a pond, mating and laying eggs from which a new generation of red efts will hatch.

The red-backed salamander, the most recent of our amphibian visitors, was even smaller than the red eft, perhaps three inches long, though it might eventually reach four and a half inches, more than half of that being its slender, tapering tail. This little salamander is one of the rare amphibians that does not live in water, even as an infant. The gilled larval stage is passed inside the egg, on dry land, and the creature emerges from the egg as an air-breathing, minute replica of its parent.

In the salamanders you can see the course of organic evolution vividly illustrated. Though they are amphibians, like frogs, adult salamanders look like lizards. The red eft is at a stage where it still needs the water. The red-backed salamander is at the stage where it can practically do without water, like a lizard. All the salamanders had to do, really, was to spend less and less time in the water, until they were eventually able to lay eggs that would hatch into air-breathing young instead of water-breathing pollywogs. That's the stage of the red-backed salamander. In most important respects it is an amphibian no longer. It is practically a reptile, a small lizard.

The amphiuma, a very large southern salamander, looks like a fish on its way to becoming a snake. Indeed, you might mistake it for either a snake or an eel, but for the fact that it has four minute legs. These seem to be absolutely useless, a mere vestige from ancestors that walked. On land the creature slithers like a snake, but slowly and clumsily. In the water it swims rapidly, and as gracefully as an eel.

I do not believe any such creature is 'evolving' in the sense that it is turning into a new species. The amphiuma may well lose its vestigial legs eventually, but it will still be an amphiuma. The red eft will perhaps become a slightly better salamander, but is unlikely to evolve into a lizard.

People who write as though these things were happening, or even say that they *are* happening, are thinking of evolution as a process that moves by 'infinitesimal degrees,' moving ever onward from the 'lower' to the 'higher.' But does it happen by infinitesimal degrees? Well, yes, in the sense that the eft may become a better salamander by such degrees. The amphiuma is probably losing its legs by infinitesimal degrees. A thousand years from now it may have none, or they may appear occasionally as an oddity, a 'throwback' to remote ancestors. But I'm not sure that this process deserves to be called evolution in the broader sense. No new species is going to appear because of the gradual loss of organs that are no longer of any use.

In Darwin's time it was absolute dogma that evolution happened only by the smallest steps which, added together over many generations – thousands or millions of generations – resulted in a major change. Such major changes, added together, finally produced a new species. More recently we have observed major changes happening suddenly. This would have been an unaccountable mystery in Darwin's time. It is not so now. We have come to appreciate that a change in a single gene, the kind of change that might be caused, for instance, by an alpha particle or a gamma ray, can result in changes of colour or shape, the number of toes on a foot or the number of petals on a flower, not through small steps, but instantly.

The migration of a single gene from its normal place in the chromosome (the 'jumping genes' of the journalists) can also produce dramatic results. There's about one chance in a million that a gene in a grain of corn will migrate, producing corn that's black, instead of yellow. (Red and blue corn has also appeared without warning.) In 1986 a geneticist at Canada's National Research Council, working with recombinant DNA, synthesized the gene that controls the migration. This discovery may enable plant-breeders of the future to produce some kinds of mutations much more frequently than now, and so to breed new varieties more quickly. It is very useful work, but hardly revolutionary. The migration of genes is just one mechanism, among others, causing mutations. Those who hailed its discovery as the answer to the mysteries of evolution were, to put it politely, hasty.

Large, sudden, dramatic changes are most often observed in plants, though they happen in animals, too. Completely hornless deer, for instance, without antlers for countless generations, have suddenly begun having calves with antlers. If such offspring bred true they could become a new species. Notable mutations occur in things such as fruit flies raised by the millions in labs. But few of us keep captive fruit flies; millions of us raise plants. Every plant-breeder looks for lucky mutations. Together with hybridizing, they provide the principal means of producing new varieties. And it must be noted, in passing, that hybridization is not evolution, either. It often produces varieties that are more useful to humans, but they are usually sterile, and have to be maintained artificially from two or more parent stocks. If the seed from hybrids is viable, it will revert to something resembling one of its parents. The hybrids are not new or improved species, or steps toward them.

Though I'm not an experimental plant-breeder, I have observed sudden changes among plants in my own garden. One such change happened to a sweet william that I grew from seed. It had white-edged leaves instead of the usual plain green ones. This kind of mutation is so common (probably caused by a migrating gene) that hundreds of 'varied leaf' varieties of numerous species have been bred by isolating the mutants, thus preventing sexual cross-breeding, the normal process by which new types are submerged and the breeding stock returned toward the normal, or 'true,' type of the species.

Had I been a plant-breeder I would have covered my sweet william with a plastic bag to prevent cross-pollination, saved all its seed, and continued with subsequent generations, weeding out the green-leafed progeny until I had a pure strain of varied-leaf sweet williams. I did save seed from the bed, but not from the variegated plant, and I am still growing the descendants of my original sweet williams without seeing the variegated mutation again. The sweet william, being a sexual species, tends to eliminate its mutations. Sex, a conservative force, tends to return the progeny of mutants toward the genetic average. If you want to preserve a new type, it is best to eliminate sex altogether, and to reproduce by cloning, as we do with nearly all our house plants. Otherwise the new type will usually disappear. (I discuss this further in Appendix E.)

The more isolated (and the smaller) the breeding stock, the better chance there is that a mutation will survive, and the better chance there is that the mutants will evolve into a new species. Because of this, new species have appeared most frequently where populations were thin, dispersed, living in conditions where survival was difficult, and forced to resort to in-breeding. Such conditions have prevailed at many times and places throughout earth history, and are one of the reasons that evolution, in the fossil record, looks as if it happens by fits and starts.

When you have a particularly useful mutation – one, for instance, that causes a plant to set seed early in a place where seasons are short – the new type may well survive in spite of cross-breeding, because it may be the only type *able* to survive, the only type able to produce viable seed. In this way a new genotype may be established in two or three generations. It is precisely by this method that plant-breeders produce hardy northern types from delicate southern ones. They set out thousands of plants, and breed from the few, or perhaps only the *one*, that can survive the cold. Soon, they may have a peach that will ripen in Siberia or a melon that will grow in the Yukon.

Evolution of this kind can happen in wild plants almost as readily as in domestic ones, provided the environmental pressure is strong enough. Usually, of course, it is not, and the new type vanishes.

I observed a very striking mutation in a wild rose – one of those pink roses, native to Canada, that grows into a shrub about three feet tall. All such roses are five-petalled, and five-sepalled. But this particular shrub was covered in blossoms, every one of which had a fully formed sixth petal, and a sixth sepal, too. Here, again, was a change in a species that had not happened by infinitesimal degrees, but by a sudden shift to a new kind of flower. Here again, had there been any point in doing so, I could probably have established a race of six-petalled roses, a number that would be unique to the species, and to the genus, and even to the family. Not only are all roses five-petalled (or 'double' in multiples of five) but all their relatives – even those as remote as apples and raspberries – are five-petalled, too.

Sometimes you see mutations among domestic animals. We have mutant house cats in southern Nova Scotia – a whole race of cats with six or seven toes on their front feet, and occasionally on their hind feet as well. We have hundreds of such cats. They are locally famous. This mutation has survived in spite of cross-breeding and in spite of its apparent uselessness, perhaps because a few people prefer such curiosities as pets. But I'm not convinced that it will survive forever. Our own cat has at least one or two six-toed ancestors, but she had been bred six times, and had raised about thirty kittens before she had one with six toes. Then two were born in a litter of five. The environmental pressure in favour of six toes is not very strong, and the odds are against an established race of six-toed cats.

On the other hand, you can observe a very useful mutation that happened in the Newfoundland water dog, and that survived to become a dominant trait. Somewhere among the ancestors of this animal one was born with webbing between its toes. Such mutations are not all that rare. Humans are sometimes born with webbing between the fingers, but since this is no advantage, it disappears again. Among the water dogs, who spend much of their lives swimming in surf, webbed feet were a powerful advantage indeed. Nowadays, *all* such dogs have webbed feet, and perhaps the webbing has been improved, over the generations, by infinitesimal degrees, but it didn't start that way. It started with a sudden genetic shift. The characteristic became so strong in the Newfoundland water dogs that it has been successfully transmitted to at least three other breeds of retrievers, all of whom are now born with webbed feet, setting them apart from other breeds of dogs.

The water dogs, in fact, have many characteristics that tend to breed true in spite of mongrelizing. They freely interbreed with all sorts of mongrels in Newfoundland and Nova Scotia, and they keep coming up water dogs, just as true to type as if they had been carefully raised by breeders in a kennel. They are an excellent example of a mammal that has experienced various fortunate mutations for which the evolutionary pressure has been so strong that they tend to survive the most persistent sexual suppression. The mystery is why the 'lucky' mutations happened so often, while 'unlucky' mutations in the same animals are comparatively rare. The water dogs have not quite developed into a separate species, in spite of the evolutionary changes. They may look like seals, but they are just as truly dogs as any other breed.

This kind of evolution is similar to what might be happening to the red eft or the amphiuma – a change that makes it a more efficient dog, rather than pointing in the direction of a new species. Only very plastic, and very generalized, types can evolve into new species. The more specialized an animal, the less possible is radical change, so that very few species indeed can contribute directly to the flow of organic evolution – less than one species in a thousand, I'm sure. But all can contribute, and indeed do contribute, to the slow evolution of the biosphere of which they are a part, and it is this contribution, every bit as much as organic evolution, that creates the flow and direction of life as a whole.

12

Creatures of the Sixth Day

The black and gray squirrels common in most Canadian cities do not live in Nova Scotia. Here we have only the smaller red squirrels, which are rather more attractive little animals, and much less likely to damage gardens. Red squirrels are one of the delights of the countryside.

These kitten-sized creatures make good use of their limited intelligence. They are smart enough to make friends readily with humans who will accept and feed them; they are also smart enough to recognize a full-grown house cat as a deadly enemy, and a half-grown one as harmless. But their instincts are very peculiar, leading them to do things that are sometimes quite silly.

Before we had finished building our house the squirrels arrived and began picking up crumbs from our deck.

'Worse than a rat fer gnawin',' a dour old neighbour warned us, but we ignored him, and left small bits of food where the squirrels would be sure to find them.

After a few weeks they brought their half-grown young ones to visit and to share the treats. We gave them mostly whole-grain bread with wheat germ, soy flour, sesame seeds – the kind we eat ourselves – and they obviously loved it. Soon they were arriving for breakfast each morning, and if Corky didn't hurry outside with a slice of bread they'd be up on a window ledge clamouring for attention. Before long they were coming inside the house, and if you were careful not to frighten them with sudden movements, they'd take a piece of bread out of your hand.

One day in autumn, immediately after a screaming battle which we heard going on in our orchard, but did not see, they disappeared. We thought perhaps the whole colony had been killed by a fisher or a marten, both of which roam our woods, and either of which can kill every squirrel within its range. They were gone all winter, and we mourned them as 'missing believed dead,' but in spring the same squirrels returned. No trouble to tell they were the same animals: they came straight into the house and began hunting for food, and walked up to us to accept bits of bread.

Giving squirrels the run of your house can cause problems. On one occasion a squirrel got trapped between the window of my newly built office and the sheet of construction plastic with which it was covered. He soon attracted my attention by screaming and chattering. He was obviously in a panic, and I had either to pull off the nailed battens, or to reach in and capture him by hand. He didn't want to be captured. He clearly felt trapped, and any attempt to help him seemed to make him even more frantic. I reached in cautiously. Would he bite? I certainly thought it likely. I slipped my hand under his small furry body, and could feel him trembling: fear? rage? how could I tell? But instead of biting he grew quiet, and allowed me to draw him out through a hole in the plastic. Did he know I was trying to help? Perhaps he was reassured by his sense of smell – the smell of a hand from which he had often taken food. In any case, the minute he was free he leaped off my hand and went tearing up the stairs to the deck, scolding as he went.

Individual pairs of squirrels treated our deck as part of their territory, and no matter how plentiful the food might be they'd quarrel with any other squirrel who came to share it: the only acceptable guests were mates or half-grown young; let a third adult arrive, as one often did, and there'd be a screaming, chattering, swearing match, often ending in a chase. The third squirrel would get its share of the food all the same, simply by dashing in, seizing a piece, and dashing away with it. All the yelling and chattering and chasing achieved nothing except a great waste of energy.

Once when we were sitting on the deck we heard a noise from the kitchen and discovered that a squirrel had managed to knock down a loaf of bread from a shelf. We watched to see what she'd do with it. She didn't try to eat the bread. Instead, with immense labour, she began dragging it toward the sliding glass door. After a while she got it there. Then she tried to pull or push it over the sill, first from one side, then from the other. She was determined to take that loaf of bread off to a cache under the deck boards or among the nearby rock piles. But the sill defeated her – she never did get the loaf over it to the deck. You'd expect her to try tearing off chunks. But squirrel intelligence evidently doesn't extend that far. Squirrels will tear off pieces they want to eat, but seem not to have learned that you can tear off pieces and carry them away with you. What a strange limitation! After a while she simply abandoned the job as hopeless, and left the loaf on the sill intact, hurrying off in search of something more stashable.

Red squirrels store things all over our property, and not necessarily in a central place. They have dozens, or perhaps hundreds, of caches, and probably put away a lot of food that they forget all about, thus unwittingly feeding the mice, the beetles, and the ants. They seem to store food indiscriminately, in any hiding place, and discover it just as indiscriminately when they're hungry. In autumn they pick up the windfall apples that the bears have missed, and take them into trees, jamming them into the crotches of limbs, or sticking them on sharp twigs, if these happen to be handy. The habit is clearly useful. The recovered windfalls will remain easily available even if there is deep snow, and are far less likely to rot in a tree than on the ground. We have never seen squirrels take the apples to a central tree, where they'd be easier to find and recover – but then, perhaps a central store would be more likely to be raided by crows or jays.

The strangest miscarriage of the caching instinct happened one afternoon when we had gone off to the beach leaving a large batch of freshly baked cookies on the table. The smell was too much for the squirrels. When we returned we found that they had entered the house by tearing a hole in a plastic screen. All the cookies were gone.

'Surely they couldn't have eaten them all!' Corky exclaimed.

I was making myself a cup of tea.

'No, I guess not. But see here – they've stuffed some of them on the shelf behind the plates.'

That was just the beginning. They had cached cookies behind the clock. Later that evening I went downstairs to my office and took a book off the shelf. Out fell a cookie. I looked further. There were cookies behind books on all the shelves. The squirrels had taken cookies to any place in the house that looked like a hiding hole. Such industry! At least half of the five dozen cookies had been taken downstairs, obviously one at a time, and carefully secreted behind books. So much for the 'infallible' instincts of animals.

All our opening windows had come with fitted screens. So had the sliding door between the living-room and the deck. All the screens were made of woven nylon. There's a contemporary fad among manufacturers for using this stuff; it's cheap, easy to handle, and customers are supposed to be too ignorant to know that it will shortly self-destruct (not to mention accidents from kids, cats, dogs, and squirrels). Those little imps soon learned that nylon screening was no real obstacle, and we had to go to a lot of trouble to replace it with wire.

Sadly, the era of squirrels sharing our house came to an end. Our kids demanded a kitten. Corky, believing that pets contribute to children's emotional development, supported this demand. And, of course, a kitten grows into a cat. Our first kitten died of gastroenteritis (caught from a visiting child) before she was old enough to be interested in squirrels. The next one reached adulthood in late autumn when the squirrels had left for their winter quarters in the deep woods between here and Porter's Point. In early spring, before the squirrels returned, he went roaming off in search of a mate and was killed on the road. Our third cat grew into an enthusiastic hunter. Before she was fully grown she had attacked, killed, and dragged home a varying hare larger than herself. From an early age she took an interest in squirrels, but the squirrels ignored her until she was more than half-grown. Then one day she chased a squirrel under the boards of the deck, where he hid in such a state of panic that I had to pry off a board to get him out.

I don't know how squirrels communicate. They do have a lot of vocal sounds, quite a large 'vocabulary,' but that may not explain how they manage to warn one another that a place they all formerly frequented is no longer safe. In any case, from the day the cat chased the squirrel, not one of them came near our deck again. We scarcely even saw one cross the yard, much less enter the house. They stayed in the ravine or the woods, and taunted the cat from the safety of the trees. I felt sorry about this, sorry that cats and squirrels don't mix. Personally I'd much prefer the squirrels. But the kids prefer the cat. You can't pick up a squirrel and maul it, and talk baby-talk to it and make it growl and purr by turns, and take it off to bed with you, and generally make a silly fuss over it, the way you can with a cat.

And then came the winter of 1987. In January, for the first time in several years, we had hard frost. In February the frost continued, and snow lay deep on the ground right through the month. It was a tough time for birds and small animals. And one day when the temperature was around -15^0c, with a bone-chilling northwest wind, we heard a scrabbling at our window-pane.

'Hey!' Corky shouted, 'there's a squirrel.'

Sure enough, after four years' absence, one of the squirrels had returned, and was asking for food. Our cat, who hates the snow, was spending the winter indoors. Two or three days later the squirrel was joined by his mate, and the two of them kept coming to the window for bread as long as the cold weather lasted. We were pleased, indeed, to know that they had lived through the intervening years and still remembered us as their friends, though we could not give them the run of the house as before.

Besides red squirrels we have woodchucks, flying squirrels, and chipmunks, none of which has ever come very close to the house. A chipmunk spends some time in our peach orchard, and a woodchuck has been known to sit on a rock wall, watching our activities in the garden. I find it hard to explain why none of those animals has ever done serious harm to our crops. Perhaps the odd peach gets stolen. If so, we don't miss it. The rodents do not gnaw holes in our squash or melons. Nothing eats our peas. People who make endless war on small animals complain all the time of their depredations, but the same creatures hardly ever bother anything we plant – and we plant everything.

We have had a few ears of corn taken by some animal that knows how to pick it – perhaps a raccoon. But the raider came only once, did little damage, and left our corn patch alone for the rest of the summer. White-tailed deer often walk right through our gardens. Occasionally one of them crosses a patch of growing vegetables, leaving small, deep footprints, but they always seem to cross from one woodlot to the other without stopping to browse. The only damage we've suffered from deer was a few branches of one peach tree, far less than we'd suffer in any late-summer windstorm.

I can only speculate that gardens surrounded by wild land, both woodland and meadow, are *ipso facto* surrounded by wild crops, the natural food of the wild animals. Aside from a short windbreak to protect young peach trees, we have never erected any kind of fence, but a neighbour of ours considered it necessary to build a nine-foot barrier to keep the deer out of his cabbages. He allows hunters on his land; we do not. Deer walk through our ravine every day of the year unmolested. Bears come here to eat windfall apples. We've even seen a bobcat stalking stealthily along the fringes of the woods. The only protection we've found necessary is for young fruit trees, which may be gnawed by mice or rabbits if their stems are left unwrapped in winter.

So generally we manage to live at peace with whatever wild animals choose to share our land, but not all of them are willing to live cheek-by-jowl with human neighbours, even tolerant ones who respect the rights of other species. Before we came here this land, and the shoreline on either side for a mile or more, was empty of human habitation. Hunters came prowling, of course, but nobody had lived here previously. And among the residents was a family of otters, living among the big boulders of our beach, and fishing just off our shore at high tide. They must have been greatly upset when we pitched our tent within ten feet of spring high water, and began building campfires among their rocks. Long before our house was started, the otters had disappeared. They waited until they were convinced that we'd come to stay, then departed for less crowded surroundings. We were sorry to see them go. We could have gotten along very well indeed with a family of otters.

Their smaller relatives found us less objectionable. Mink, marten, and ermine weasel all manage to tolerate us. Andrew and Leah once watched a weasel catch a mouse right under their noses. The little animal popped out from underneath the very boulder they were sitting on, snatched the mouse off the beach, and dashed back under cover, all in a matter of about two seconds. Then, with the mouse safely stashed, the weasel came out again to have a look at the two children sitting sky-high on the roof of his house. His curiosity satisfied, he then went back under the boulder to enjoy his meal.

So far as we can, we do not molest the creatures that share our territory. I have chased deer and rabbits out of the garden now and then, or frightened off a flock of crows when they showed too lively an interest in our germinating corn or peas. Generally, though, the crows would rather forage in our compost pile than in our corn patch. In any case, it's easy to protect sprouting corn with Styrofoam coffee cups, giving it a head start, as well as protection. Once it's two inches high the crows won't touch it.

I'd chase a bear out of the yard, too, because bears that hang around houses can become great nuisances, and might well be dangerous to children, but the ones around here don't need to be chased. They are so ruthlessly hunted that they stay well out of the way of humans, and tend to visit orchards only when the owners are asleep.

There are many reasons why we do not allow hunting on our land. We want the animals to stay here, to feel at home. We regard hunting by civilized men as a perversion. Man is not a predator, and is not descended from predators, as I explain at length in a later chapter. Unlike a cat, he does not hunt from instinct. In civilized places he does not hunt from need, either. In a few places (the Arctic, for example) a very few people hunt from necessity.

I must mention my own hunting, or someone will accuse me of hypocrisy. I did some meat hunting, years ago: caribou and seals, mostly in the company of Inuit hunters in Labrador, but also in Newfoundland. I never, at any time, hunted birds or small 'game,' never hunted for sport, and have not owned a gun of any kind for nearly twenty years. But I regard meat hunting as respectable, a thing I'd do myself without feeling demeaned. Sport hunting, on the other hand, is contemptible. In our society people hunt mainly from lust. Hunting, to put it in plain language, is most often a form of sexual perversion, like rape or child abuse, and it's damn well time we faced the fact, and called a spade a spade.

I do not, obviously, accept the old argument that we should make 'wise use' of other species of mammals. To me they are not 'natural resources' to be 'managed' by departments of game and fisheries and the like. This may have served for the ethics of a previous generation, but it is an extension of the medieval view that everything was 'made for man's use and benefit,' the view that god created 'the beasts of the field and the fowl of the air' specifically to be exploited by humans. I cannot accept the proposition that there is any such thing as 'wise use' of other species of wild animals. Nothing less than respect for their rights will do.

Rights? Rights. The world belongs to them, too. They have made the journey, as we have, through some four billion years of struggle toward the light. Each species has taken a different road, and it so happens that the road we have taken has given us control over awesome powers of destruction. All the more reason we should be cautious how we use such powers. All the more reason we should develop a sense of responsibility not only toward our own species, but toward all others, and toward the fabric of life itself. There is no way I can see a licence to kill for pleasure as being any part of a sense of responsibility toward nature, toward the world, toward the universe. The gun is a toy that we are eventually going to outgrow.

13

Majesty in Blue

The heron looks black as he cruises above our treetops, or moves over the clam flat with a slow pulse of wings, searching the creeping tide edge for a likely spot to land. Like an osprey or an eagle, the great blue heron conveys a sense of being fully in control, at one of life's peaks, and though we've seen them a hundred times before, we still call excitedly to each other or to the children when one flies close to our window. Seen close up, while standing immobile, waiting for a fish, the great bird is at least as magnificent as it is in flight: large and graceful, elegantly plumed in an array of soft colours: pale lilac, dove gray, soft cinnamon, and snowy white – hues visible only at close range in good light. When we see them far off, ranged along the edge of the incoming tide, they look the way they do in flight – as black as crows.

Because I lived most of my life in a land where the great blue heron is a rare visitor, the sight of this handsome bird alighting on my front lawn is still able to make me catch my breath. Why the lawn? It seems to prefer the clam flat, and after that the ponds in our ravine, but after watching its activities at every opportunity I discovered that it does not feed exclusively on fish and frogs. Sometimes it hunts on land. It won't pass up a small snake, or perhaps a vole, if one comes scurrying past, and I've seen it in the meadow among the clumps of goldenrod and dusty asters snapping up grasshoppers by the hundred.

The herons of Annapolis Basin arrive singly in the spring and depart in flocks in the autumn. In September or October we often see as many as twenty standing like sentries along the mile and a half of tide line between Porter's Point and Ryerson Brook. They are monuments of patience. They seem to spend their lives just waiting. You usually have to watch a long time before you see one make the lightning thrust by which it catches a fish.

Then one day they vanish, flying off like migrating geese in a V-formation toward Cape Sable and the crossing of the Gulf of Maine. Occasionally a single bird remains over winter. I've seen one on the Fundy mud flats in February, braking in flight to alight between the ice pinnacles left behind by the enormous tides, searching for the burrows of marine worms, or the breathing-holes of the soft-shelled clams. Its companions of the summer, tenants of the marsh-ringed heronry where they nested in a dense colony, had departed long since for New Jersey, Virginia, the Carolinas, or the Gulf of Mexico. They would not return until April beckoned the spawning fish toward shore. Then the great blues would come planing out of the sky, scattering around the edges of the Bay of Fundy and northward through Cape Breton Island, a few of the most venturesome finally crossing the Gulf of St. Lawrence to western Newfoundland and the salt marshes of Bay St. George.

The famous naturalists Audubon and Bent, who shot birds by the thousands for museum skins, or in order to record their 'food habits' by poking around in the contents of their crops, regarded the great blue as suspicious and wary and difficult to approach. Audubon and Bent would have been difficult to approach, too, if those approaching them had been armed with guns, determined to kill them. But this bird, like the Canada goose, soon learns the places where it is not molested. I've frequently had close encounters with great blue herons, not by sneaking up on them – that indeed might be difficult – but by behaving myself in plain view. I've stood on the bank of my own pond watching a heron catch tadpoles and water bugs not fifteen yards distant, and have seen one beside my front door, teetering on a wire overhead, wondering if it ought to fly, because it wasn't quite sure it could trust me, though I had never offered any heron the slightest offence.

Like every large bird in North America (and many small ones) the great blue formerly suffered frightful persecution from sports. I mean frightful, not merely widespread. An atrocity. Herons were never regarded as game birds, and were rarely eaten, but great blues were left to rot on the ground by the thousands after sportsmen had enjoyed the fun of killing them and the pleasure of watching them die. The gunners usually shot the great blue herons on their nests, and since they nested in dense colonies, the laughing sportsmen were able to murder entire populations all at once. Presumably most such sadistic slaughter is now over – we have at least learned to call this kind of sport by its proper name: a hideous massacre.

In the upsurge of spring, filled as it is with love and rivalry, great blues engage in spectacular sparring matches that can only be compared to the symbolic combat of caribou stags. I've watched a pair of rivals on the sand spit at Goat Island rushing at each other with beating wings, fencing furiously with their deadly beaks, one thrust of which, in neck or breast, would instantly kill a competitor. They rushed about like a pair of Valkyries, and one expected to see blood and feathers, at the very least, scattered about the field of battle. But then, in an instant, it was all over. One of them, perhaps losing heart, perhaps physically exhausted, crouched on the sand in humble submission while the victor strutted in glory. A moment later the loser got up and slunk away unhurt. Then he made a little flight to the far side of the point, alighted, and began to preen his feathers. Not a scratch on him. I've never known a heron to be killed in such encounters. I've never seen one actually hurt. I can only lament that human rivalries are not settled like this by a bout of karate where all punches are parried or pulled harmlessly a hairsbreadth short of their mark.

Why must we kill each other, while the great blue herons can resolve their disputes in symbolic jousting? I believe the reason is precisely because we have no natural weapons with which to kill. The heron, armed from birth with a murderous spear that could impale any other heron with ease, brings into the world with him an instinctive taboo against killing other herons, against using this deadly weapon to murder those of his own species. Humans, with no natural killing equipment, descended from millions of generations of unarmed anthropoids, invented killing at such a late date in their history that they have not had time to evolve taboos against destroying other humans, and consequently are now in danger of self-extermination, as the herons might have been had they evolved with the beaks of sparrows and then invented spears.

Konrad Lorenz observed, many years ago, that predatory animals have a taboo preventing slaughter within the species. They have an inability to kill those of their own kind who submit, or engage in 'appeasement ceremonies.' But such unarmed creatures as turtle-doves, kept in close confinement, may disembowel one another. If you have to face either a deer or a wolf in a cage, you are much safer with the wolf, so long as you know the appeasement gestures.

Besides the fencing matches, herons have another spring ceremony: communal dances, courtship rituals in which dozens or even hundreds of them gather on a sand spit or a mud flat to execute in concert a stately saraband. The rivalries are now over. The pairs are wedded. They come together for a communal celebration. The herons dance in couples, circling with outspread wings to the drumming of an inner music. Then they disperse two by two to their nests. But they rarely nest in solitary pairs. Usually they collect in colonies of at least a few dozen birds, often with a number of nests to a single tree. The colony on the fresh-water island in the beaver meadow overlooking the Bay of Fundy has about thirty pairs, and doubtless there are others, smaller and larger, within a few miles of the shore of this great bay.

Like ravens and ospreys, the herons prefer to nest in tall spruces, or in mature firs or hemlocks; indeed, there is an osprey's nest on the same island as our heronry, and ravens occupy a tall, lightning-blasted tree no more than a quarter of a mile away. Those large birds do not exactly share their nesting territory in peace; rather, they share it in a state of armed truce. The ravens try to steal the herons' eggs, and the herons try to steal the ospreys' food – none of this with conspicuous success, but all of them forever on the alert. The larger the heron colony, the safer it is from ravens and other nest-robbers, because when a heron discovers a predator near its nest, it promptly screams for help, and all other herons within earshot come hurrying to the scene, primed for battle. An angry heron is a formidable creature, and even a lynx would probably flee if faced with more than two at a time.

The habit of calling in the neighbours to help drive off predators is not peculiar to herons. Farley Mowat once took a film-maker who was visiting him from Hollywood to see the nest of a Canada goose on a beach near his home in Port Hope, Ontario. He knew that ganders will usually try to defend their nests and their mates, and was much surprised to see this one flee headlong from the scene as they approached, while the goose remained, crouched low over her eggs. But the gander was gone only a minute or two before he returned – with another gander. The two birds then flew straight to the attack, screaming and hissing with fury – and Mowat and his visitor beat a hasty retreat, leaving the beach to the geese.

Nest-robbing aside, the great blue heron has nothing to fear from any other bird. No hawk, not even an eagle, would dare to attack so large and well-armed a creature. No four-footed predator smaller than a wolf would choose to face it, either.

The large herons are a clear illustration of the combined principles of co-operation and competition in nature. Both work to their advantage: sexual competition, and communal co-operation. Naturalists of only two or three generations ago, trying to see everywhere a fierce 'struggle for existence,' would have tended to overlook the co-operation, or to dismiss it as unimportant to the great scheme of evolution. But in fact it is at least as useful to the species as are the sparring and the dancing in the mornings of early spring.

We often see in the world around us what we are predisposed to see, and overlook or misinterpret all that fails to fit our preconceptions. We think in models or paradigms, fitting the chaos of observation into some kind of pattern. Such patterns may change, not quite so rapidly as the fashions in dress, but rapidly enough so that totally opposed pictures are accepted in the course of a single lifetime. Social and economic systems affect this process, and even 'objective' science falls under their influence. Thus, in the nineteenth century, and in the early years of the twentieth, when capitalist economics were regarded as immutable – indeed, founded in the laws of nature – nature herself was regarded as fiercely competitive. So we had every individual for himself, and the devil taking all but the foremost, not only in the industrial cities, but in the forests and the deserts and the seas. Nature was red in tooth and claw, and woe betide him whose teeth were not the longest. Individuals struggled with each other for food, for mates. Species fought against species for living-space. Perfection emerged from fratricide at home and genocide abroad. It was assumed without investigation that *Homo sapiens* had killed off all earlier human species, if they hadn't killed each other off beforehand.

It was a fierce picture, one that justified by analogy human warfare and the rise of the Nordic myth, one that justified ruthless economic exploitation together with the neglect and even the persecution of the weak. By extension, human affairs should be left to run themselves competitively, the efficient company gobbling up the weak one, the fast worker paid to set a killing pace, the slower gradually starving, and women and children savagely exploited. The most cunning, the most ruthless, were engaged in carrying forward into a bright, fiercer future the competitive scheme of things that god had wisely ordained for this planet and its living freight.

In our time a strongly opposed view has almost managed to become orthodox dogma: the 'web of life,' the concept of nature as a vast co-operative commonwealth ruled by the New Democrats, with everything working together in mutual support, forming a complex and extensive living system, a balance of nature in which no wrong can occur so long as humans do not interfere.

Occasionally, man was included as part of the commonwealth, but only so long as he remained at the Inuit or Bushman level of culture, immersed in nature and living with it in a sort of religious symbiosis. Mostly, humans were regarded as dangerous outsiders, likely to wreck the beautiful pattern, to tear the web, to destroy the balance, dragging the ruins down around themselves like rabbits released on a tropical island by early mariners, eating every green leaf and sprout and finally dying of starvation in a foodless desert.

This view of the balance of nature became popular at the same time as co-operative economics, mergers, price-fixing, 'managed' national economies, the welfare state, and the belief that the human community is a mutually supportive unit rather than a struggling chaos in which the fittest will survive.

Neither view by itself is correct. Each has elements of truth. Nature indeed is co-operative in the broad sense. The fox is not the enemy of the rabbit. Had there been foxes on the tropical island in my example, the rabbits would probably still be there. The red-in-tooth-and-claw picture hardly fitted herds of gazelles grazing peacefully alongside whole clans of lions lying at ease in the sun, paying no more attention to the gazelles than to the cloud shadows sweeping over the veldt. On the rare occasions when a lion gave chase, there was indeed an element of competition: the swifter gazelles were more likely to escape.

And then lion-watchers observed that it was not just the swift and fierce lions who filled their bellies. The groups (called 'prides' by hunters, for some imponderable reason) acted as co-operating units. Lions that did not make a kill got food from those who did. Only lions belonging to a strange tribe would be driven away from the common meat supply. Where was the fierce, internecine competition that ensured the survival of the strongest? Not among lions, apparently.

But there still remained the sexual struggles, those fights to the death between males, rivals lying dead all over the place, while the victors strutted off with the nubile fillies and filled them full of sperm. An arousing picture – until field researchers observed that most male animals were more likely to compete by dancing than by fighting. In many species there was little evidence that stronger or smarter individuals were more likely to mate than weaker or stupider ones. Moreover, wives were exchanged like chattels, and sometimes husbands, too. The harem with its antlered lord, the noblest surviving stud, turned out to be a male-chauvinist myth. In fact, the entire picture had been built up by naturalists sitting in their studies writing books, based on imagination rather than on field notes.

Perhaps we are closer to the truth than our elders, but we'd be rash to assume that we are very near it, even now. The 'balance of nature,' that darling of the conservationists, is beginning to slip from its intellectual pinnacle. It now seems that what nature manages to achieve, fairly often, is not balance, but a kind of rough compromise in a state of flux, with many species constantly vanishing from whole areas, or even from the face of the earth, with invasions and expansions, and nothing remotely resembling a divinely ordered welfare state. If nature is not red in tooth and claw, neither is she parlour pink.

Everything about the natural order is more complex than we could have imagined possible in the simple world of our schooldays. Until recently there was a near-universal habit of reducing things to simple models, usually mechanistic ones. Such models are still useful, so long as we remember that they represent only a minute fraction of the underlying reality. A heart, for instance, is a pump. But also much more. Perhaps it would not be wrong to say that it is infinitely more.

The concept of the balance of nature belongs in the same category of reduction. It is a crude mechanical model. Nature appears to be in balance only if we freeze it into an abstract state, like a photograph of a runner in mid-stride. Moreover, the connections of this changing system are not closed or limited, but open and infinite. The so-called ecosystem of the tidal flats and salt marshes, where the great blue heron spends its summer, is intimately and obviously connected with the moon, and much less obviously with the geology of Mars, but it is also connected by routes that we do not yet begin to understand with an underlying matrix of life in other eras and other places. Taking any part of nature and describing it by a mechanical model of interacting parts is like the famous walk-in model of the cell – almost laughable, nowadays, in its reductionist absurdity.

I recently sat at a 'campfire circle' in a national park and heard a wildlife officer deliver a lecture with slides on the balance of nature, cautioning us that everything in the park must be protected from human interference, even the insects and the micro-organisms and the rotting wood on which they live. And I thought to myself how absurd this dogma sounds to one who has lived immersed in nature for half a lifetime. For the dogma exists only because the human animal is seen as exterior to nature, as one of the poles in a man-nature polarity. And this, in turn, has come out of the old Semitic dogma, adopted into Christianity, that man is a special creation, not a part of nature, but distinct from and superior to it.

Of course I do not claim that because I am human, and a part of the ecosystem, this gives me the right to drain the salt marsh indiscriminately, or to mow down the trees on the island in the beaver meadow, and evict the great blue herons from their nests, leaving desolation behind me. The powers we have, though they do not place us outside nature, do saddle us with responsibility for their use. But neither do I feel much sense of guilt when I burn a dead tree, robbing the fungus of its food and the ants of their city. I even feel that I have the right to make my own niche in the world quite large and spacious and comfortable. I believe nature, in its perpetual state of flux, will make an eddy to accommodate me. The universe has no dead-end roads. You can't create them, even with a bulldozer.

14

The Meadow and the Shore

It is Indian summer, a season filled with the riches of the year, and looking at the meadow overflowing with goldenrod and Michaelmas daisies, a riot of lavender and gold, I find myself wondering again how to explain the miraculous achievement of the plants, the glory with which they have clothed the earth. Flowers are among the very recent products of terrestrial evolution. Life flourished on earth for billions of years before the first flower burst into bloom. They look like what they are: one of the highest expressions of life.

Explanations are offered (of course). You can always find people ready to explain anything, usually with simplistic arguments. Some people will tell you that the clothing of the grass of the field in raiment more glorious than Solomon's is a mere matter of cross-pollination. The range of colour and form in the world's flowers, all their subtleness of shape and scent, amount to nothing more, we are told, than an advertising gimmick, designed to attract winged customers to anther and stigma. Indeed? And isn't it the strangest coincidence that this appeal to the senses of fly and bee should appeal so profoundly to humans who have no wish to sip nectar or collect pollen?

Why, indeed, are we attracted to flowers? They do not look or smell like food or sex or anything else that would support our survival. They appeal to us in ways that mean nothing to those who explain sunsets in terms of atmospheric dust, or birdsong as the mere marking of territory. I suspect that there's more to the glory of the plants than meets the first simple probing of the human mind. Their achievement is as astonishing, in its own way, as the human achievement of orchestral sound. They have done with colour and form and texture something as remarkable as what we have done with music. And perhaps for a similar reason. Music and flowers are aesthetics that stand alone, possibly unique in the universe, but unique or not, reason enough in themselves, without utilitarian explanations. Explaining the subtleties of an orchid in terms of seed production is like explaining Mahler's Eighth Symphony in terms of a mating call.

Unlike Darwin, I do not regard flowers as 'an abominable mystery,' just because their explosive appearance so late in life's process cannot be explained by natural selection alone. I regard them instead as a glorious mystery (to borrow a term from the outmoded discipline of theology), a demonstration that life draws great draughts of inspiration from sources that we cannot see through our microscopes.

I don't think Mahler's late symphonies can be explained by natural selection, either. I think trying to explain such miracles by such a simple theory is like trying to explain the Taj Mahal with a slide rule. It is one of the major achievements of our time, of these latter years of the twentieth century, that we have recaptured mystery and magic, and regard them as sacred rather than abominable.

There is more mystery, more beauty, more wonder abroad than we were taught to believe in our outdated flirtation with mechanistic rationalism (the Newtonian 'death' of Blake's polemics). I believe I'm rational, but I hope I'm not simplistic. The mechanical model that held sway over men's minds from the time of Kepler and Newton until Einstein turned it into shimmering fireworks was a vast oversimplification of what is, in fact, an infolded subtlety, a subtlety built layer within layer, becoming more subtle and more complex the deeper we probe. And if this is true of the physical world, it is true in an even deeper sense of the world of life. The idea of the universe as something like a steam engine, to be explained in a few pages of mathematical symbols, was in retrospect so simplistic as to be absurd. Only incredible arrogance wedded to vast ignorance could have led us to such conclusions; yet they have been widely accepted, and sometimes are accepted even now among doctors of philosophy and fellows of royal societies. Moreover, they are widely assumed by millions of 'lay' people who believe themselves capable of thought. Many of the unspoken assumptions behind our social and political structures stem from the exploded dogma that the universe is a clock.

Flowers have not been free from the human urge to meddle with anything that can be shaped, altered, or 'improved.' Those in our gardens and greenhouses have mostly been changed by our interventions into something 'closer to the heart's desire.' We have selected them, cross-bred them, hybridized them, subjected them to all the minor devices of organic evolution that we have learned how to manipulate, though we still cannot control the great evolutionary forces, those by which species leap out into the dark, and are transformed. Even so, our horticulturists may not be quite the magicians that we sometimes suppose, for many of the world's most spectacular flowers continue to look very much like their relatives in southern China, the Amazon Basin, or the foothills of the Himalayas. No human influence has affected the lovely Victoria lily or the stunningly beautiful Jimson weed. They selected themselves.

Watching the blossoms of the red clover in my meadow bend under the weight of the bumblebees, I marvel once again at the way plant and insect are fitted together, hand in glove. It would be equally wrong to say that the bee has adapted itself to the clover, or that the clover has adopted its present form to suit the bee. Both, in fact, have evolved together, grown in partnership over millions of years. Bee and clover, and all the other elements in the ecology of the meadow, have developed out of the roots of life as a connected, functioning system, every part affecting the development of every other, the whole of it striving toward a greater perfection, toward a more intricate complexity, toward a more perfect fit into the external environment that all together must share, succeeding, very slowly, in making even those external conditions better suited to their needs. For even such remote systems as rainfall and cloud cover are modified, to some extent, by the clover and the bee. The sky is blue, and not yellow, because they live on the surface of the earth.

It is obvious, once you think about it, that species do not evolve in isolation. You might almost say that species, as such, do not evolve at all. What evolves is a complex system of interconnected life together with its environment – an ecosystem. Each creature modifies its surroundings, including the external environment and the creatures with which it interacts; life and the non-living world evolve together. And when a new species appears it is not so much because a previous one has been developing in a particular direction, as because the biosphere has changed ever so little, and by that change has made room for something that did not exist before.

Yet much as this, once stated, may seem a truism, it has been overlooked by most of those who turned their minds to the problem of life's becoming. Even so great a naturalist as Rachel Carson, writing of rock periwinkles, described them in *The Edge of the Sea* as 'poised . . . in time, waiting for the moment when they can complete their present phase of evolution and move forward onto the land.' The rock periwinkles are not evolving into land snails. Far from it. To the extent that they are changing at all, they are fitting more and more perfectly into the splash zone, the zone where they now live, the region of the shore that is wet with spray and slippery with the microorganisms on which rock periwinkles feed. The whole ecosystem of the splash zone, like that of the meadow, is changing, but so slowly that we cannot guess what is happening to it. A billion years from now neither the meadow nor the shore will have the same life forms, the same chemistry, the same colours and shapes that it has today; life will have passed on to new complexities; the bee, the periwinkle, the clover, the algae will all be embalmed in the segment of time that we call 'the present.' They will not have moved forward or upward or downward, but there will be new species of living creatures, evolved in partnership with each other and with the changed world that the bee, the periwinkle, the clover, and the algae helped to create.

Some writers, anxious to see in evolution the working out of a vitalistic determinism, have described life in the sea as pressing relentlessly forward to the land, always in the one direction, urgently fulfilling its destiny. This, of course, is a romance. There's no mystery about it. Since the sea was filled with life while the land remained relatively empty and seemingly hostile, there was no other direction in which life could 'press.'

I have given my reasons elsewhere in this book for believing that life evolved many times, and not only in the sea. But there is no doubt about the fact that the sea was populated by complex, highly evolved animals and plants, long before such creatures lived on the land. The land, a much harsher environment than the sea, remained *relatively* unpopulated, while the sea became crowded, all its environmental niches filled with appropriate life forms.

So life crept forward, inch by inch, into this relatively empty space, precisely because there was room for it to move in that direction; not because it was beckoned thither by some divine destiny, but because there was no other way for it to go. Had the land been populated first, and had the sea remained for long unfilled, life would have pressed downward just as relentlessly into the splash zone, into the intertidal regions, down through the plankton layer and the mid-ocean twilight, and finally into the abyssal deeps. We must not create mysteries where none exists; there are enough of them remaining in the universe to occupy our minds forever; we do not need to gape in wonder at those things we can already explain.

As I look about me on the Annapolis shore, in its meadows, its woods, its tidal reaches, and its waters, I find a great many things that I can explain, much of the wonderful surge of life that fits into a pattern in time and space. I see life evolving in an orderly way because no other way was possible, and I see it interacting with itself, with its myriad parts, in a harmonious pattern, not because someone worked out the puzzle in advance and ordered things according to natural 'laws,' but simply because no other pattern would do. Life does what it can, all the restraints being what they are, and does it extremely well.

There are, too, many things I cannot explain. I think I know how stars are born – something my grandparents could not know. Perhaps my grandchildren will know how this universe came into being, something about which we can only speculate in our time. Meanwhile, the parts of the cosmos that I can perceive are not a chaotic mystery, as they were for nearly all the years that have passed since humans began to think and reflect and inquire.

I know little about the beginning or the end of that universal order of which I am a part, but this I know: it is not running down or expanding into nothingness as the prophets of entropy and black holes and the like would have us believe. To think it could be so is the ultimate romanticism; to believe it is to propose God the Creator fashioning universes *ex nullo*, blowing bubbles and watching them disappear, a myth fully worthy of Omar Khayyam out of Edward Fitzgerald. If it weren't for its elements of the tragic romance, the black hole would be the perfect symbol for our time, and no doubt that's why it's so popular.

All this, of course, is no proof. No *reductio ad absurdum*. It may satisfy no one but me. Others, if they wish, may believe in the Potter and the broken pots. I am unable to do so. I simply know that the true story of the universe is not a tragic romance: when and if we come to understand it, it will have neither a mythic beginning nor a wildly tragic end; it will flow rationally, like a river, like the story of the bee and the clover that has, in fact, no beginning except in our imagination, and no end except that which we may arbitrarily assign.

The meadow and the shore are not only overflowing with riches in colour and form and music, but with such variety of living creatures as might occupy the whole life of an observer. In the five or six acres that lie between our house and the shore there must be thousands of species of insects, some hundreds of species of plants, and perhaps fifty species of birds, not to mention the amphibians and the reptiles and the small mammals that are mostly concealed from sight by the vegetation.

Apart from flowers, the birds are the most conspicuous, some of them clothed in defiant colours, as though scorning the cheap devices of camouflage in a world where 'carrying the flag' may be more important than hiding from harm. Redstarts, goldfinches, bobolinks, to mention only three of the commonest birds of the meadow, fill the air not only with bold patterns of flashing colour, but with loud and continuous song. Such birds have no intention of crawling into a hole and drawing their pensions.

Birdsong is no mere 'argument about real estate,' as Sally Carrighar expressed it. Birdsong is basically territorial; we can consider that proven. But the territorial instinct has been elaborated into complex and beautiful music, just as the territorial arguments of nation states were sometimes elaborated into poetry. It does not seem strange to us that humans should sublimate their baser instincts into art. Why should it seem strange for birds to do so? The song of the hermit thrush, a spiritual outpouring that seems to make a statement about the bird's relation to the cosmos, may have had its dim archaic origins in the idea of territory, just as the lofty poetry of the prophet Isaiah had its origins in the narrow concept of a small nation and a tribal god. It is the grand achievement of the songbirds that they have reached a level of art which speaks not to their own species alone, or even only to related species, but to creatures as remote from them as mice and men, an achievement that must be reckoned among the peaks of terrestrial evolution, like the achievement of the flowering plants, and the vocal systems of the great whales.

It took computers to analyse the perfection of birdsong, to reveal to us that birds reach a refinement of pitch beyond that of the most sensitive human ear, and (this should be a lesson in humility) that when they imitate human music, as they often do, they amend its imperfections, altering our gross approximations to the refinement of perfect pitch that they take for granted as the heritage of every creature with hearing.

As the meadow gives way, through a narrow strip of salt marsh, to the sand and rocks of the shore, the bold contours are muted, the music is stilled. One would hardly describe the calls of gulls and terns and most shorebirds as music. The bold colour of the blue-flag iris and the riotous pink of the morning glories and wild roses are the last statements made by the meadow, before the muted subtleties of the shore begin.

Sea lavender blooms abundantly among the salt grasses, and even among the rocks, but you must almost get down on your knees to appreciate its beauty: it has none of the riot of the asters or the goldenrod, but a rarefied delicacy of form and colour. Seaside goldenrod blooms all through the salt marsh, and well out into the sand, but it is small and inconspicuous compared to its giant relatives of the meadow. The rock pools give the shore its greatest charm, but here too muting and subtlety are the rule. The plants and animals are small, though their forms often seem to come out of some realm of fantasy. There the small algae flourish in soft purples and reds. Mussels and periwinkles add muted blues and ochres, while small sea anemones contribute pastel shades of peach-pink and ivory. Jellyfish sometimes spread faint iridescent rainbows, which flicker for a moment, then vanish with the changing of the light. The whole of it is a kind of jewellery, fascinating to see, very fragile, slow-moving, attuned to the slow-paced rhythms of the sea, and contrasted in almost every way with the humming, bustling, brilliant life of the meadow.

I never see such fragile forms of life without feeling the weight of responsibility that has descended upon humankind in this century for the first time in our long history. Everything that lives, whether of the meadow, the shore, the forest, or the further wastes of the earth, has now fallen within our keeping. We can destroy it all, if we will. We never before had such awesome responsibility. In former centuries we might, it is true, exterminate a species here or there; we destroyed the great auk, the wood buffalo, the passenger pigeon, the Eskimo curlew, and the Labrador duck, but our capacity for destruction was limited to this or that species. Now, with the rise of technology, with our ability to alter the very chemistry of the sea, or of the earth itself, with our capacity to poison the air or to bring on a nuclear winter, we are quite suddenly responsible for the well-being not just of ourselves, our own future, or the future of this animal or that bird, but of the entire biosphere, the intricate and marvellous structure of terrestrial life that has been growing and developing, becoming more complex and beautiful around us for a period longer than our imaginations can encompass – a period measured in billions of years, while the continents formed, the rocks were laid down, and the oceans rose and fell in the incredible geologic dance that is linked to the planets, the stars, and the galaxies.

Though we are obviously living in the period of greatest danger for ourselves, for the earth, for all the life that we know, though we are living in a period of human madness that could bring the evolution of life on earth to an end, I am encouraged by the numbers of people, still small, but growing all the time, who feel a sense of responsibility toward the world, people who, while yearning for the human childhood that ended a generation ago, are convinced that humans must now become responsible adults, must not bring to an end the glories that the plants have created, the music of the birds, the subtleties of life along the shore and in the tidal pools.

At the same time I am horrified by the small-mindedness of the world's rulers, most of whom continue to think in the categories of the human childhood, in terms of 'national security,' in terms of sovereign states – men who can place life-and-death issues like acid rain in the balance against such trifles as economic ups and downs, men (and women) who can even contemplate a world-wide nuclear holocaust in the foolish belief that a few of them, if lucky, might inherit the cinders of a ravaged planet.

15

Hawks at All Seasons

Just above our beach on Annapolis Basin, barely out of reach of the highest tides, stands a fine old birch surrounded by aspens and pin cherries. Here, both summer and winter, a red-tailed hawk likes to perch, surveying the beach on the one side, and the cranberry bog on the other, with the kind of imperial hauteur that only hawks can achieve.

We have often seen this bird take prey from the beach, less frequently from the bog, and never out of the air. It seems to be attracted only by things on the ground, mice or shorebirds, or perhaps snakes or frogs or salamanders (though it would look in vain for those in winter).

Sometimes it soars far up, watching through telescopic eyes the small jungle of the grasses, seeing the telltale movement of mouse or vole or savannah sparrow that no human eye could discern from such a height. Then it plummets suddenly to earth, and if its attack has been successful, it may just stay there and enjoy its meal among the beach peas and the sea lavender and the goldenrod.

Almost two feet long, and armed with powerful talons, the red-tailed hawk sits serene at the upper end of the food chain, unbothered by fear of any serious attack. The crows do not chase it, the way they would chase an owl, and mostly it enjoys its haughty perch in tranquillity, preening its feathers and stretching one wing after the other at those times when it has nothing better to do.

Strangely enough, small birds do not seem to fear the hawk unless they are on the ground, when, of course, they had better watch out. I have seen two blue jays sharing the same tree with the red-tail, obviously unconcerned except that they regarded the much larger bird as a proper subject for harassment. They would perch a few branches away, then swoop up, one at a time, and come diving down at the hawk, missing him by a whisker, actually brushing his feathers once or twice as they swept past. The hawk put up with this for a while, then shook his feathers out and took a leisurely departure for quieter surroundings, much as a man might move away from a pair of yapping pups.

I have also seen a flock of evening grosbeaks alight unconcerned in the tree next to the one where the hawk was perching. But in spite of their boldness I noticed that they were careful not to occupy perches lower than his. Like the jays, they treasured their altitude, and it occurred to me that perhaps no small bird has any great fear of a hawk except when the hawk is overhead. For instance, they reacted quite differently when a merlin (pigeon hawk), another of our winter residents, came falling like a tiny thunderbolt out of the sky, heading straight for their tree. Though the little falcon was scarcely larger than the grosbeaks, they scattered in panic and dived for cover into the thick brush.

Because of its interest in things on the ground, and its habit of soaring, the red-tail was often shot as a 'chicken hawk,' but perhaps not so often now that chickens are only rarely exposed to the sky. This persecution, and the pesticide poisoning that so often killed embryo hawks while still inside the egg, has reduced the red-tails to a mere remnant of their former numbers, but in spite of everything they have managed to survive better than their relatives, the red-shouldered and broad-winged hawks.

The red-tail loves to soar. Its eyes are so keen that it can see prey on the ground from great heights, but it often seems to soar more from the love of soaring than from any need to hunt. Andrew and I have watched a red-tail spiralling upward in a thermal current higher and higher over the shore of the basin until the bird with its four-foot wings was a mere speck against piles of cumulus clouds. Then it began to flicker in and out of sight along the edge of vision, and finally vanished into the blue and white of the zenith. It is hard to believe that the hawk could see a vole among the grass and wildflowers at a distance where we could not even see the hawk, but apparently it is so.

It must be a thrilling experience to soar like that, higher and higher into the great vault of the sky without having to do more than alter the pitch of wings and tail to catch the currents of the air and rise free among the embryonic thunderheads. The bird on the rising air is enjoying an immediate, physical adventure within the great soaring adventure of life, and knows this perfectly well, not as a symbol in its head, perhaps, but as a dancing fire in its whole being.

If I owned chickens and suspected that they were threatened by hawks, I'd go to the trouble of covering their runs with wire before I'd even consider shooting a red-tail. It kills, yes, like many other animals – and like Shiva, that archetype of human myth measuring out the paces of the dance of life. As so often happens, our myths are wiser than our intellects. Humans were worshipping Shiva the Destroyer, and picturing him as sub-limely beautiful, one of the aspects of the creative trinity, thousands of years before they understood the tragic but essential truth that death is an inextricable element in the creative force of evolution. The myth of Shiva is infinitely wiser than that crop of researchers currently busy in America trying to find a way to put an end to human death, to stretch life to indefinite limits, to bring human evolution to a stop.

Nova Scotia is the northeastern limit of the red-tail's range, though in Quebec and Ontario it penetrates further northward. It is therefore somewhat surprising to find this bird at Annapolis Basin in winter, especially since southern New England is often said to be its northern limit in winter. I suspect that its winter migrations are dictated more by scarcity of prey than by any desire to escape the cold. In regions of heavy snowfall, where prey animals rarely come to the surface in January or February, red-tails would likely starve, as other hawks sometimes do. I once found a dead merlin frozen to its perch in a tree, presumably a victim of winter starvation. In the Annapolis region, where the average snowfall is only ten inches, and where in most winters the ground is bare or nearly bare much of the time, a red-tail can make a somewhat precarious living even in January and February. Perhaps the dangers of remaining so far north are no greater than the dangers of migration, during which even strong birds can be swept away and wrecked by storms, or brought low by the caprice of hunters and farmers, many of whom shoot hawks every time they get the chance.

In summer we occasionally see a Cooper's hawk, a sharp-shinned hawk, and, fairly often, a little kestrel (sparrow hawk). We have not had a peregrine falcon in the Annapolis region during my seven years' residence here. This is the bird of prey that is closest to extinction in eastern North America. Bird-watchers here may pursue their hobby for decades at a time without ever seeing this splendid falcon, formerly the favourite of kings.

Among our permanent residents is a pair of northern harriers (marsh hawks). They are sometimes here even in winter, flying back and forth over our cranberry patches in search of small animals. Marsh hawks are exceptionally handsome creatures, the male gray and rather gull-like, the female larger, and spice-brown, both with bold white rump patches. They sometimes fly so low while hunting that we actually look down on them from our deck, which is about sixty feet above the level of the beach.

Voles, snakes, frogs, the occasional muskrat, and small ground birds are among the marsh hawk's prey. Like many of the raptors, it will steal prey from other species if it gets the chance – even sometimes from the large falcons.

In early spring the marsh hawks fly like ravens, rolling and somersaulting in the air, diving in great swoops almost to ground level, staging prolonged exhibitions of aerobatic skill. Most of the performers are males, as you'd expect, showing off for their lady friends, but females do it too, on occasion.

So far as I know this is the only hawk that nests on level ground. Some others nest on ledges or cliffs. The marsh hawk seems to prefer the cover of shrubs or small trees, but sometimes it will nest on a dry hummock in the middle of a marsh. I have not seen a nest at Annapolis Basin, but there has to be one not far from our house each summer, for we always have a mated pair of marsh hawks in May, June, and July, often hunting together. Later in the year there may be two or three immatures, but only fully adult birds seem to remain over winter. I'm not sure, of course, that the pair we see in winter is the same pair we see in summer. Marsh hawks commonly migrate over long distances; those that winter here could be visitors from Newfoundland, or even from southern Labrador.

In February another pair of visiting hawks arrives – goshawks, perhaps coming down to the shore to hunt when the pickings have been lean along the heavily forested South Ridge, a piece of wild territory where they generally feel more at home. Those gray marauders of the airways are the only birds that fill me with a sense of evil. Silly as it may be, I can't admire a goshawk or feel a thrill of empathy when I watch it pounce, as I can when I watch a falcon fall out of the sky, or see a buteo soar from sullen earth toward heaven's gates. The goshawk is a savage and methodical killer, the Nemesis of the far north, the predator that most often attacks such large ground-dwelling birds as grouse, ptarmigan, and pheasants. It appears not as a distant speck falling out of the sun, but in a low-level attack over the tops of the nearest trees, a tactic exactly like that devised by low-level bombing planes to avoid detection by radar.

When I first saw two goshawks hunting along the shore of the basin on the eighth day of February I wondered whether they were a mated pair. It seemed likely. They were hunting close together, and one was a little bigger than the other. The bigger bird would be the female, about half a pound heavier than her mate. Perhaps they associate all year long. Perhaps, like geese and swans, they mate for life. Unlike ravens and owls, which begin nesting in midwinter, goshawks do not begin their breeding cycle in Nova Scotia until the first flowers appear in spring, but those two looked as if their association might have lasted at least since the previous summer.

Early in the nineteenth century goshawks were much more plentiful than they are now. In those days the immense flocks of passenger pigeons (running into the *billions*) provided them with unlimited prey. The pigeons migrated south for the winter, but only a short distance. Their winter range extended into the northern states, and hawks had to fly south only a few hundred miles to continue exploiting this plentiful prey. With the extermination of the incredibly abundant pigeons many birds of prey, including the goshawks, began starving to death, failing to raise their young, and this process continued until their numbers were down to something approaching their present level: from having been common birds, they became relatively rare.

The goshawk does not confine itself to such easy prey as pigeons. This powerful killer will attack almost anything, even other birds of prey, including birds as large as itself. Crows, ravens, and owls have all been found dead in goshawk nests.

I have seen a goshawk chase a whole flock of crows that I would have thought were more than a match for it, had they chosen to mob the hawk as they would have mobbed a fox or an owl. Instead, they scattered in panic in all directions, and the goshawk, having missed his first strike, perched in one of our cherry trees while the crows fled out of sight.

An American farmer once reported that he had found a goshawk and a barred owl (a predator about the same size as the hawk) both dead on the ground in February after a fierce battle in which blood and feathers had been scattered widely over the snow. In a sense the owl had 'won' the fight; it was only recently dead, still warm, while the goshawk was frozen stiff. It is not surprising that a bird so courageous and so well-armed as the goshawk will sometimes attack humans in defence of its nest. But then, so will marsh hawks, great horned owls, bald eagles, and even common terns, which are hardly bigger than jays. The courage of nesting birds is not something to be trifled with.

This was the only hawk that regularly raided chicken runs (in the days when chickens ran), sometimes carrying off full-grown hens, and earning for itself the more or less deserved name of 'chicken hawk.' It is hardly surprising that pioneer settlers with their little subsistence farms and their half-dozen hens running around in the back yard learned to hate this hawk with a real passion. Unfortunately, they transferred their hatred from the goshawk to all other birds of prey, most of which are quite innocent of raiding farmyards.

The goshawk is not an arctic bird, like the gyrfalcon and the snowy owl, but it nests north to the limit of trees in Labrador, and westward along the edges of the barren lands to Alaska. Here in Nova Scotia we are near the southern limit of its nesting range. A hundred years ago nests were found in the northern states, but only rarely, even then. I have heard of none in recent years.

Like the other large birds of prey, the goshawk suffered devastation when humans exterminated its prey species, and again when they began recklessly spraying DDT and other chlorinated hydrocarbons over North American croplands. But much of the goshawk's summer range was wild, even 'unman-aged' forest land, beyond the fringe of human settlement in Canada, and in such unpoisoned regions the goshawk has continued to flourish. But there is no guarantee for the future. If the pulp and paper industry is allowed to have its way, the forests will be turned into poisoned cropland, not only throughout the Atlantic provinces, but eventually all the way north to the limit of trees. If that happens, all the large hawks may become extinct in Canada as well as in the American states.

On a bright morning in December a bald eagle came soaring over the basin, majestic in its white head and tail feathers and its almost black body. People call it the 'king of the birds,' but not all birds regard it with respect, despite its size and power. This particular eagle was invading territory along our beach which is 'owned' by a greater black-backed gull and a flock of crows. They all became greatly upset by the presence of the invader.

The crows set up a great clatter but carefully kept their distance. Not the saddleback (as the fishermen call him). He hurled his goose-sized body courageously into the air and made straight for the eagle in a power dive. The eagle circled, and circled again, alternately flapping and soaring, but the saddleback, a marvellous flyer, managed to maintain his position always a little higher and a little to the rear of his much larger opponent.

The crows, meanwhile, did not dare to try mobbing the eagle, but simply formed an aerial cheering section, far enough away for safety, loudly urging on the saddleback to more vigorous attacks. Finally admitting defeat, the eagle ceased to circle, and headed off over Goat Island in the direction of Digby, the saddleback following at greater and greater distance, eventually returning to soar in triumph over his domain, to which peace and the long-established hierarchy had been restored. While the saddleback soared, the crows settled in the trees, exchanging little cawing sounds, congratulating one another on a job well done.

The falcons, harriers, and buteos are true predators, specialized for hunting. They require meat to keep them alive. They occupy among birds the same place as the great cats among mammals, and as the sharks among fishes. Among mammals there are lesser predators, such as weasels and foxes, and half-predators or scavengers, such as dogs and jackals. Among birds there are shrikes and crows and gulls. These are the lesser predators and scavengers.

Where do humans fit into this picture? Not at all. Biologically, man is not even a jackal, much less a tiger.

16

Of Men and Hunters

On the day in early autumn when the season opens for hunting small game, Annapolis Basin resounds with the booming of guns. The smell of smokeless powder drifts across the water. The Great Goat Island Rabbit Drive has begun.

In years when the population cycle is near its peak, Goat Island raises a bumper crop of varying hares. The reason may simply be the island's fertility and isolation. Sealed off from dogs and foxes and bobcats, none of which would choose to swim across the tidal streams that separate the island from the mainland, it shares the good soil and long growing season of the Annapolis region, and has a bountiful supply of everything from clovers to spruces. It is a place where hares may safely graze. Until open season. Then in a single day some eighty per cent of the hares are converted into meat. Half of those remaining will later join their cousins in the cooking-pots.

Then the deer season opens, and to go into the woods is to take your life in your hands. You aren't safe even driving along the road in a car. One woman had both back windows shot out of her car last year. An accident. A teenager, sitting out in the open on a tree stump the year before got a bullet through his heart. Another accident. I sometimes venture into the woods at that season with a chain-saw, because I find it hard to believe that even deer hunters can hallucinate a deer operating a chain-saw, but I still don't feel safe. Rifles spit lead on all sides up and down the shore. Two or three boxes of shells go up in smoke for every deer that inhabits these woods. Fortunately the one thing few hunters seem able to do is shoot straight.

Hunting, among the small minority of human males who actually do it, amounts to a religion. This activity, above all others, sets them apart as men. If they happen to be Protestant fundamentalists (as many of them are) they'll quote the Bible, telling you that Nimrod was a mighty hunter before the Lord, and that man was given dominion over the beasts of the field and the fowl of the air – 'dominion' in their sense meaning a licence to kill.

If they happen to be able to read books they'll tell you that man is a killer ape, an instinctive predator, that for untold generations he hunted meat to feed his mate, and his mate's cubs, back when he lived in the caves. Even today, they will tell you, a real man still has the instinct to go out and hunt red meat for his family.

I began questioning this 'instinct' myth many years ago while all the anthropologists were still talking about the human 'hunting phase,' and calling man a predator. The habit of scepticism that has been with me since childhood prompted me to ask certain questions:

1. If humans are predators, if they had a long line of predatory ancestors, then why are they the only predators in the world who need daily rations of vitamin C in their diet?

2. If humans are predators, why does a diet rich in animal fat give them heart attacks?

3. If humans are predators, why don't the females, as well as the males, have this instinct to go out and shoot red meat? In real predators the females are at least as good at hunting as the males, and usually better. *They* are the ones who hunt to feed the cubs, and often their mates, as well.

4. If humans are predators, why don't they have any of the natural equipment of predators? Why do they have the teeth

and the metabolism of fruit-eaters rather than of meat-eaters?

All attempted answers to such questions, and many others like them, seemed to me to be no more than clumsy rationalizations advanced to support a preconceived notion.

Certainly there have been human hunters. There still are. A few people even live by hunting. For a few small tribes it was once the principal means of livelihood, but really for very few. It seems doubtful, to say the least, that hunting could have had any major effect on human evolution, that there was ever such a thing as a 'hunting phase' for more than a small fraction of our ancestors, or that there is anything remotely like a 'hunting instinct' in either male or female humans.

I have lived to see many anthropologists come around to my way of thinking. Some of them may have learned some biology, but the thing that is changing their views most rapidly is the accumulation of human and pre-human fossils dating back over a period of some four million years. These fossils lend no support to the idea that man, at any stage of his development, was a killer ape, or that *any* carnivorous ape ever existed.

Humans were prey, not predators. They were once food for the great cats. Overcoming this condition, escaping from the status of a prey animal, was perhaps the greatest of all thresholds in human evolution.

As for my neighbours the hunters, I note that there are no females among them, and only a few mature males. Several years ago I happened to be skiing cross-country with six other men, all from this area, when we came upon the tracks of a coyote, and drifted into a discussion of the animal's status. To my astonishment I found that not one of the seven of us owned a gun. In other respects we were a cross-section of the local male population. The only things we had in common were a fondness for the woods and for skiing, and a dislike of hunting.

Most hunters seem to be young men and boys still unsure about their own sexuality, the same class for whom automobiles are a sex symbol and a rite of passage. Hunting, in our society, is tied into a lot of cultural lumber much closer to backwoods Kentucky than to any cave man. And we are getting rid of it, slowly. Hunting, like smoking tobacco, is no longer quite respectable, though still a widespread addiction among certain social groups.

We have learned more about the primitive nature of man in the past twenty or thirty years than in the whole period since Darwin. Among the things we have learned is the danger of projecting our myths and our cultural prejudices into the past. It has become clear from the new evidence of the archaeologists, as well as from a new examination of facts previously known, that the old view of the Primitive Hunter, the vision of man as the Greatest of the Carnivores, was never anything but a romantic myth, dear to the macho hearts of male primitivists.

Some of the myth-makers, projecting their theories into the remote past, saw a pre-human phase even earlier than that of the hunter. They saw man's tree-dwelling ancestor, some tens of millions of years ago, as a 'nocturnal insectivore,' a creature who, because of his insatiable urge to wander and to conquer new territory, came down from the trees and set off across the savannah, stone axe in hand, to butcher his first bison and to enter his hunting phase.

The only part of this that will bear close examination is the coming down out of the trees. At a remote period we did indeed live in trees. And at some stage we gradually spent more and more time on the ground until we became ground-dwellers. But the rest of the theory faced a range of unanswerable questions even before the *coup de grâce* was delivered by recent fossil discoveries:

Why should man, any more than the other anthropoids, have been a nocturnal insectivore? If he was nocturnal, why does he have such poor night vision and such fine colour discrimination? Why don't his eyes resemble the saucers in the faces of owls and nocturnal monkeys? If he was an insectivore, why doesn't he synthesize vitamin C, like all other insectivores? Why, in fact, does he have the dentition and metabolism of a fruit-eater?

It is now clear that humans were never insectivores, and never graduated from insectivores to carnivores, and that only in a few specialized places (the Arctic, for example) did they depend upon meat as their primary source of food. It is quite clear that pre-agricultural man was for millions of years a forager and food-gatherer, just as he still is in those few places where he is not farming or herding animals: in the deserts of Australia and the Kalahari of Africa, for example. Food-gathering tribes today do some hunting, as most human tribes did in the recent past, but it is, and always was, a secondary activity, invented at a late stage in human development after the invention of effective weapons. Such weapons, weapons that could be relied upon to supply a tribe with meat, were invented 'only yesterday,' much too recently to have contributed to our store of instincts.

The image of primitive man as a hunter comes from one limited race in one region: the Neanderthals of ice-age Europe and Asia. The Neanderthals, who are now regarded as a race of *Homo sapiens*, not as a separate species, were specialized in many ways for the rigours of their environment. They had large, thick-set bodies, and abnormally large brains, they dressed in animal skins which they cut and sewed into fitted garments, and they were hunters. They were, in fact, a very specialized fringe group of humanity, the Eskimos of their era, living at the limits of the habitable world, hardly a part of the main line of human evolution. Their contemporaries in Africa and southern Asia, the principal ancestors of modern man, were much like we are today: smaller, slighter, less specialized. They did not wear animal skins, or any other clothing that we know of, and hunting was but a minor part of their overall economy.

Then, following the Neanderthals in Europe, there were the reindeer-hunters, the Cro-Magnon people. They were not physically specialized, but perhaps culturally specialized, and they occupied only a tiny fraction of the earth, and a quite recent niche in human history. We do not really know how great a role the reindeer played in Cro-Magnon life, but it may well have been central to their economy, and may even have held a religious significance, as it does among the Indians of Labrador. We should remember, though, that hundreds of species of seeds have been found preserved in their caves. In any case, taking Neanderthal and Cro-Magnon together, they occupied perhaps ten per cent of the habitable earth for perhaps two per cent of human history. Those percentages put hunting into its proper perspective as a late and relatively unimportant human activity. It *seemed* important to early anthropologists because they themselves were north Europeans, living in the little corner of the world formerly occupied by the specialized hunters, and (like Freud and Kinsey and many others) they projected the traits of their little corner of the world across the whole of humanity.

The 'hand axe,' one of the most widespread artifacts of the Old Stone Age, pictured in numberless fanciful paintings of packs of cave men pursuing their prey, was not a weapon at all, much less a weapon capable of killing a mammoth or a bison. It was a tool, like our axes of today, and was doubtless useful for cracking bones or butchering a carcass, if you were lucky enough to find one or to trap one in a snare, and for a host of other chores from splitting kindling to building a shelter. But it was just about as useful as any other chunk of rock to a hunter pursuing live prey.

Sticks were undoubtedly used by humans ages before they began shaping stone axes, just as sticks are used by chimpanzees today. Sticks were not only the first tools, but also the first weapons. They are not very effective weapons for hunting, but they are excellent as a means of defence, which is one of the ways in which chimpanzees use them. You can sometimes fend off a leopard with a stick, and it becomes even more useful if it is sharpened to a point in a fire. The first human weapons were weapons of defence.

The spear-thrower, the bolas, the bow and arrow, all became effective hunting weapons, but all were recent inventions, products of the last few thousand years, as compared with the millions of years that men have been walking upon the earth.

Even in warfare the spear was essentially a defensive weapon, and that is certainly the way it was used in the Old Stone Age, and long before that. It was one of the principal human defences against the great cats, some of whom, even now, have not thoroughly learned the lesson that humans are too dangerous to be treated as prey, and who – Indian tigers among them – may well be facing extinction because this knowledge is coming to them too late.

Much nonsense has been written not only about the Archaic Hunter, the Predatory Ape, and so on, but, as an inevitable result of such myth-making, about the Agricultural Revolution as well. This was always a problem for those believing in predatory apes. Why, in the name of heaven, did the Mighty Hunter begin growing wheat? Can we imagine a tiger with improved intelligence speculating on the advantages of growing grain? But that's exactly the picture we were offered. The hand that had picked up the stone, ages before, and dreamed it into a weapon, now plucked a handful of grass seed, and held it contemplatively, dreaming of something that might replace the diminishing supply of meat.

Of course, nothing of the kind ever happened. Once we realize that humans of the mainstream were always food-gatherers, living mainly on fruits and nuts and grains and roots, with shellfish as a staple if a tribe lived beside the sea, and the meat of birds and small animals when they could get it, then the difficulty of the Agricultural Revolution completely evaporates. The metaphorical tiger never had to begin dreaming about growing wheat, because he was never a tiger.

Agriculture arose naturally among food-gatherers. It happened over thousands of years, not in a swift 'revolution.' It began when seeds gathered for food spilled and germinated around camp sites, at first sown by accident and, when this proved profitable, by more and more care and cultivation. Even today waste seeds grow abundantly in dooryards. Tomatoes are one of the principal weeds in my flower beds. Cross-pollinated squash keep coming up around my fruit trees, sometimes bearing large, edible gourds of a type never seen before. Because fruits, nuts, grains, and roots were the staple human foods at every stage of human evolution, no forethought was needed, no contemplation, no revolutionary insight, in order to develop agriculture. It just happened, over long periods, and is still happening, even today. As the products of cultivation gradually became the principal source of food for a tribe or band, it was inevitable that the tribe or band should lead a more settled life, gradually evolving into the population of a village, a town, and a city.

Looking back into the distant past is something like using a very long telescopic lens to photograph a distant scene. It collapses and foreshortens the background, so that we tend to see things that happened over thousands of years as sudden events. Thus we get expressions such as 'the revolutionary change in food production that took place in early neolithic times,' and we may well forget that 'early neolithic times' refers to a period perhaps as long as that from the pyramids to the present. Once we get back beyond *written* history, a few millennia here or there seem to make no difference, and we can easily accept a change that took place gradually over thousands of years as 'revolutionary.'

But all truly revolutionary movements have been recent. You could speak of an 'intellectual revolution' in Greece, since it occupied no more than two or three hundred years. The European Renaissance might properly be called revolutionary: it took place within a century or so. The industrial revolution occupied about two centuries. The electronic revolution began in the middle of the nineteenth century, and is still going on. In the distant past the 'revolutions' were developments spread over vast stretches of time. Agriculture very slowly replaced food-gathering. Bronze very slowly replaced stone. Iron replaced bronze, not in any sudden sweeping movement, but bit by bit over centuries and millennia. The Iron Age began in

Europe perhaps four thousand years ago, but Europeans were still casting bronze cannon in the time of Columbus. This revolution, like the others before it, was spread over thousands of years.

Perhaps fifteen thousand years ago, if not earlier, a few people were already sowing seed. The practice spread very gradually. There are still whole tribes of people living today who rely on wild roots and seeds for their principal food supply. But inexact as the term may be, we'll doubtless go on referring to the Agricultural Revolution, because many important changes were connected with the rise of agriculture: the growth of flocks and herds, the demand for pasture, the appearance of towns, the rise of walled citadels, the founding of the first small 'empires' that were able to include more than one village or town or tribe in their domain, and, not least, the rise of organized warfare.

There was doubtless some fighting and killing in pre-agricultural times, perhaps even something like the raiding and skirmishing that went on between Indian tribes in North America before the European fur trade organized it into warfare. But so far as we have been able to observe them, nomadic tribes of food-gatherers have not been found practising anything resembling warfare in our sense. Raiding for profit, communal fighting, the profession of the soldier, the organized army, all came into being after the rise of agriculture and the evolution of towns and cities. Warfare is only loosely connected with primitive aggression. It is a *civilized* activity, rarely undertaken for instinctive reasons, nearly always with the clear motive of profit, be it loot, territory, or trade.

It is easy to see how an animal that began using weapons for defence against predators, as the great apes use sticks and stones, and slowly improved the weapons until they were useful not only in close-up defence, but also for killing at some short distance, would have gradually learned to hunt small game. The spear-thrower has an effective range of twenty or thirty yards. As the weapons were further improved, and especially after the invention of the bow, men began to hunt larger and larger beasts until even the bison did, in truth, become human prey for a very short time in the very recent past. But this happened much too recently, I must repeat, to have implanted hunting instincts in our chromosomes: only many thousands of generations can implant a new instinct in an animal that is not descended from other animals with similar instincts.

Far from being instinctual, hunting is nothing but a cultural trait handed down from father to son, from uncle to nephew, and from older to younger members of the peer group. I have discovered in my own children not the slightest urge to hunt or kill anything. Quite the contrary: they are horrified by the idea of killing. The men who pursue rabbits and deer so avidly through the woods around Annapolis Basin are all men who have taken their culture from older hunters, clan leaders. There is a whole class of other youngsters who have not been subjected to such brainwashing, and who have no wish to chase and kill animals. A ten-year-old neighbour of mine whose father is an avid hunter assured me that he never in his life intended to hunt anything. Perhaps he will be shamed out of this soft, unmanly attitude when he begins running with the teen-age pack, but if hunting were instinctual, ten-year-olds would already be feeling the urge. A kitten will chase prey even before it is weaned.

I thoroughly believe hunting to be foreign to man's nature, a late cultural experiment that has no basis in the genetic code, any more than it has in the code of chimps and gorillas, our closest relatives. Chimps will eat a small rodent if they catch it, or a small monkey, but have neither the urge nor the equipment to hunt in any serious way. Such instincts are the heritage of true predators like the cats, remote from our line of descent.

So far as the record can be read, there has never been a predatory ape in the whole history of the anthropoid group, or in related apes and monkeys. Even those best equipped for hunting, the long-fanged baboons, which are only distantly related to humans, eat meat on but rare occasions. They are omnivorous food-gatherers, living on fruit, roots, bulbs, insects, and eggs. The long fangs of male baboons are for defence against leopards, their most persistent predator.

The males of most ground-dwelling primates are much larger and better equipped for fighting than the females, and in fact act as defenders of females and young if the band is attacked. Male baboons are much larger than the females, have a thick mantle of fur for a shield, and have canine teeth three times longer than their mates. Among humans there is a striking lack of such extreme sexual dimorphism. The human male is only slightly larger than the female, and has absolutely no specialized equipment for fighting. The human, in this respect, is like a tree-dwelling rather than a ground-dwelling primate, and it seems that such masculine specialization as exists – a slightly larger and stronger body, a bearded, and hence perhaps more frightening, face – must be the vestigial inheritance from remote ancestors rather than an adaptation to the specifically human state.

Humans must have developed their specialized means of defence at the same time that they began living on the ground. Otherwise, they could not have survived. A tree-dweller who came down and began running about on all fours, no better equipped than we are for fighting, would have been eaten on the spot.

The specialized human defence consisted of large brains, sharp sticks, and fire. We already had the upright posture, because we had been standing upright in trees for several million years gathering fruit from the topmost branches. We already had the opposable thumb and the grasping hand, the specialized equipment of a fruit-picker. The idea that the hand and the weapon evolved to fit each other is another myth that we can ignore. If you've ever picked fruit by climbing trees you'll know exactly why we have the upright stance, the reach, and the grasp. One of our very early fruit-eating ancestors has been identified in the fossil record: *Aegyptopithecus*, a small, ape-like tree-dweller that lived in North Africa thirty-three million years ago.

Those who tried to make the hand evolve to fit the weapon, and the upright stance to free the hand so it could hold the weapon, had their chronology all backwards. It should have been no surprise that 'Lucy' – the oldest ground-dwelling human ancestor yet discovered – was found walking upright more than three million years ago. There was not the slightest evidence that any human ancestor had walked on four feet at any time since the first one ventured to run from tree to tree and scramble into the branches. It was simply *assumed* that we must have walked on our knuckles in the clumsy manner of the gorilla before we walked straight. (But we have none of the vestigial knuckle-pads that should still be there had this been so.) Had we been forced to evolve the grasping hand to hold a weapon after we were already living on the ground, we would have been extinct long before it had ceased to be a paw. But because we had the hands of fruit-pickers we were able to handle sticks, and even to throw missiles, as tree-dwelling monkeys do, long before we ever arrived on the ground. And that happened only when we were ready to defend ourselves against the dangers of the ground.

It would be silly to think of the descent to the ground as a sudden occurrence. It is quite possible that our ancestors were already using fire before they completely abandoned the trees. They must have lived on the ground for a long period while still using trees the way squirrels use them: as a place to sleep, and a place of safety when pursued. Climbing trees when threatened by bigger animals may still be instinctive in humans.

Fire was an even more powerful defensive weapon than the stick. It could successfully fend off a tiger, even while the fire-maker was asleep. As I write, we still cannot trace the origins of fire-making, but I am reasonably sure we shall find proof, eventually, that proto-humans armed themselves with fire at least four or five million years ago.

We first used fire for warmth, and for defence against

predators. Defence against the great cats was vital in the struggle to survive. Cooking was a mere frill. If creatures on the borderline between ape and human used fire millions of years ago, it was not to cook meat, of which they had little or none, but to escape their fate as prey. With fire and a wooden spear, ages before the first 'stone tool industry,' man was no great hunter, and was far, far from being 'the most aggressive carnivore the world has ever seen.' But he was well able to defend himself, and this was the crucial point: with fire, a spear, and a large brain, he had become too dangerous an animal to be regular prey for leopards and tigers, as his ancestors must have been when they first ventured out of the trees. To live in the open, humans had to be able to defend themselves. Fire gave them the means to do it.

The symbiotic relationship between humans and dogs may also date from this remote period. Dogs are scavenging animals, ineffective as predators, but their keen sense of smell and hearing make them very effective as sentries. A dog, not much good for fighting a tiger or a leopard, would be very useful in an encampment of humans armed with spears.

I saw this demonstrated not once, but time and again, by a twenty-pound female dog owned by my wife. When we camped in country where bears were common, no bear could get near our tent without the dog knowing it and setting up a frenzied barking. This would happen while the bear was circling stealthily about, silent and hidden by the trees, long before any human could detect the intruder's presence. The bears must surely have known that a twenty-pound dog, by herself, was not dangerous. Bears aren't that stupid. Yet the barking of the dog frightened off the six-hundred-pound bear without fail, because a barking dog is the symbiotic partner of an alert and armed human, who is, indeed, not a safe creature to approach, whether you are a bear or a leopard or a sabre-toothed tiger.

Humans and dogs have complementary equipment: human vision, human intelligence, human dexterity, complemented by canine hearing and sense of smell. This combination, originally of great use when humans were liable to be preyed upon by the great cats, was later very effective in hunting. Dogs, excellent trackers, were never much good as killers. Humans were hopeless trackers but, once armed with spear-throwers, or bows and arrows, were deadly in attack. So, at the times and places where hunting became a regular occupation for men and dogs, the symbiosis between the two species was further cemented.

It is worth noting that baboons have an analogous relationship with some of the ungulates. Baboons, like humans, have excellent sight. The ungulates, like dogs, have a keen sense of smell. The two unrelated groups of animals remain close together and use their specialized senses symbiotically for defence against lions and leopards.

Ice-Age Man is another persistent myth associated with the myth of the Great Hunter, and beloved by people of Nordic extraction. The English, when they were the world's top dogs, liked to be told that they and the Scandinavians and the north Germans were superior to everyone else on earth because of the harsh climate of northern Europe. There was – to some extent there still is – a cherished belief that Cro-Magnon man, the first good-looking, high-browed, nicely chinned European, had somehow emerged out of the European ice age, rather than out of a tropical jungle or savannah. He was always shown in artists' conceptions with a white skin, too. There was no evidence for this, of course, but he had to be shown as a true WASP, and always as a male.

From such present knowledge as we have, it seems that nearly all human evolution took place in Africa, and that the highest-browed people who ever lived came from south of the equator. They were even more advanced-looking than Cro-Magnon. Indeed, they resembled the fanciful pictures of future humans in science fiction, with oversized brain-pans.

If Cro-Magnon had really emerged from the ice age, he would have been covered with fur, but in fact he doubtless entered

Europe from the south. Not only did humans evolve in a hot climate, but all the early civilizations arose in regions that had never been touched by ice: at Nineveh on the Jordan, on the delta of the Tigris-Euphrates, in Egypt, and, a little later, in the Hittite region of the Near East. It is quite clear that man, including the species called *Homo sapiens*, has always been by nature a tropical or subtropical animal who penetrated the frozen regions only late in his history and only with much difficulty. The ice has had an effect on his recent culture; it played no role in his biological evolution.

A few people on the edges of the great human expansion that covered Africa and southern Asia hundreds of thousands of years ago spilled over into Europe and northern Asia, and eventually even into North America, where they did indeed contend with ice, and hunt large grazing animals between the tongues of the glaciers. A few are still doing it. But only a comparative handful of that vast, world-wide expansion ever had the experience of walking over a snowfield in pursuit of an animal, and the experience can have had little effect upon the total human emergence.

For a century and more, scientists made a great fuss over the human brain and how it developed and why it exists at all, creating another mystery where none ought to be. Why should a brain be more of a mystery than any other organ? The bat's ability to fly by echo-location seems to me an even more unlikely specialization than a high-powered brain. It is actually very simple: humans, among the least-specialized of animals, faced with the grave problem of survival in a world filled with powerful predators anxious to eat them, developed as rapidly as possible the best defence of which they were capable. Because they had no teeth or claws to speak of, no wings, and no great fleetness of foot, the available defence was brain-power.

The controversy over the evolution of the brain stems from a piece of self-deception. Minor scientists, with no gods to worship, tend to worship their own intellects. Because they can follow the logic of a few pages of math, and talk to each other in abstract symbols, they regard their own brains as almost supernatural, and go around telling us that 'primitive man' must have been equipped with this supernatural brain at a time when he had no use for it, when he had little to do except butcher his meat and dig grubs out of stumps. Such egoism! It's a pity those supermen have never had to face the problem of a sabre-toothed tiger. They'd soon find out that problem-solving is not just a matter of a few transformations in the calculus.

Darwin, equally at sea when it came to explaining how his own brain had evolved, or – much worse – *why* it had evolved, postulated a long, fierce struggle of man against man, in which all but the very brightest were killed. No evidence for such a struggle existed. Indeed, all the available evidence pointed the other way; primitive humans were highly co-operative rather than competitive. Among such primitive, pre-agricultural humans as the Australians, the Bushmen, and the Inuit, living in regions where food was scarce, the struggle for existence between man and man was unknown. But Darwin was forced to explain the evolution of the brain somehow; perhaps, he argued, at some forgotten stage humans were loners, killing each other at every opportunity. How else could environmental pressure have created the brain? How indeed!

The very same egoism that made anthropologists stand in awestruck wonder before the miracle of their own brains also made them blind to the fact that at one stage of his evolution man had been a prey animal. Such a humiliating possibility could not be faced, so they didn't even examine the possibility.

When I first took my four-year-old daughter to see a pair of cougars at the nearby wildlife park I was surprised at the way the great cats acted. Toward me they showed nothing but a mild interest. Toward my wife the same. The child, however, excited them. They lowered their heads and paced. They wanted to get through the bars so that they could reach her. They acted exactly the way I saw a female lion act in Central Park when a goat walked close to her cage. To the cougars the child was prey. It took me a while to realize this, obvious as it was, because I'd always thought of cougars as timid creatures who never attack humans. Indeed they do not, if the humans are six-footers, standing upright. It was only when I saw the same activity repeated with other small children that I began to recognize a hunting instinct in the great cats – even such 'timid' ones as cougars – an instinct that saw small humans as natural prey animals, in a class with sheep and goats. A few million years ago we were all that size. We grew, in 'Lucy''s time, to about four feet – just the right size for a leopard. We were prey.

We reversed this state of affairs. We evicted the leopards and tigers from their very lairs, taking over the caves where they had once sheltered. Eventually we sought their skins as trophies, and made them into fur coats. This struggle, settled not by growing long teeth and claws and a huge body, but by developing a superior brain, was a far greater evolutionary force than any possible struggle of 'man with man,' for which there is no evidence in the fossil record.

Again we should remind ourselves that brain-power was not used for the first time by Euclid. Had Albert Einstein lived in the Old Stone Age, would he have invented the bow and arrow? Did it take less brain-power, less insight, less imagination to invent the bow than it did to work out the general theory of relativity? I'm not at all sure that our brains were going to waste before we began juggling abstract symbols. On the contrary, I suspect that the life-and-death struggle with the predators took more brain-power than we have ever needed since. The struggle also left permanent marks upon us. Cat phobia, even of harmless creatures the size of rabbits, is still common among humans and dogs.

There were various possible defences against predation, in addition to teeth, claws, wings, and fleetness of foot. Some prey animals learned to breed at a great rate, producing so many offspring that even a small portion of them could carry on the species successfully. Humans were unable to do this. They had already chosen the route of the one-cub litter and the long gestation period coupled with prolonged childhood necessary for an animal that was developing a complex culture and cultural tradition. They needed something else, and they chose what may have been the only thing possible, a three-pronged defence consisting of a large brain, the use of the spear, and the use of fire. I believe those traits developed very quickly, and that the large brain was the key to the other two.

Chimpanzees do not have brains big enough or complex enough to conceive of the use of fire, or how to control it. It is only the lack of fire that prevents the chimpanzee from turning his stick into a spear, for a stick sharpened and hardened in the fire becomes a very effective spear indeed, even if it is not tipped with stone. There is a select African society to which you are only admitted when you have killed a lion single-handed with a spear. The lion has to be provoked into charging you, and is then impaled. The spear is still a very effective defensive weapon. And, in addition to making this weapon possible ages before men began shaping stone, fire was itself an effective defence; no predator would enter a cave with a fire burning at its mouth. A prey animal developing such previously unheard-of defences would have needed every cubic centimetre of brain capacity that it could muster. It was a world in which only the best brains lived long enough to leave descendants. The evolutionary pressure in favour of the brain was extreme.

As I sit beside a pile of blazing driftwood on the beach, contemplating the long human relationship with fire, it occurs to me that this was perhaps the crucial element separating man from ape. To sit alone beside a fire at nightfall in the wilderness is to understand the extent to which fire is involved with our deepest instincts. It is not a mere matter of warmth, cooking, comfort, safety: it is all those things, but, beyond them, it is an element far more potent in our history than the 'opposable thumb' or 'tool-making' or any of the other elements selected by anthropologists to explain the gulf that separates humans from their biological relatives.

The Greeks were right about this, as they were about so many other things. The Promethean 'gift' of fire raised man above the beasts and set him on the path leading to civilization. Fire was the basis for everything that followed: human defiance of the predators, human ability to live securely in caves or compounds, human conquest of colder lands outside the tropics, reaching eventually to the shores of the Arctic Ocean. When the primitive natives of Tierra del Fuego were first discovered they had almost nothing in the way of tools or creature comforts. They had no houses or tents. They went naked in a sub-arctic climate. But they had fire. They kept campfires blazing everywhere, all the time, so that their land was named for their fires.

Millions of years after it was first tamed by our ancestors, fire became the basis successively of the Bronze Age, the Iron Age, and the Age of Machinery. Without fire, man would have remained an Australopithecine, a very clever ape, somewhat superior to the gorilla, but still an ape. Once we had learned to use and control fire, there were no limits. We could develop culture and traditions and history, and finally expand from the earth into the solar system.

There is no fire anywhere so primal, so attuned to the human essence, as an open wood fire in the wilderness. That is the place and the condition where it all comes home, and we relive the millions of years of racial memory from the time when dark-skinned naked humans dragged great logs into their camps and kept roaring fires belching flame and sparks into the night sky, while the sabre-toothed cats skulked, defeated, in the distance, and padded off toward extinction.

17

A Festival
of Finches

A blaze of gold falling out of the sky, bolts of celestial fire – flickers of ivory and ebony – and lo! our cockspur thorn, sitting in the white glare of a February morning, is more fully alive with colour and movement and the ripple of life than ever it was in May.

'Here they come!' Corky exclaims. She sits with her morning coffee overlooking the dead meadow and the icy shore. But our nine-year-old daughter Leah has very cleverly installed a bird-feeder in the thorn tree below our window, and thus has attracted about fifty evening grosbeaks, winter birds that look like creatures straight out of the tropics, glowing as they do with yellow and green and black and white, punctuated with soft tones of gray.

I was opposed to the idea of a feeder. Much against my better judgment, we have two cats, one of whom (the female, of course, name of Catkin) is a ferocious hunter. I'd told Leah I wasn't in the least interested in attracting songbirds to our door to be turned into cat food. But as soon as she reached the age of independence she decided that the rest of us could do what we liked, but *she* was going to feed the birds.

The cockspur thorn, a beautiful tree armed with vicious spikes three inches long, was the perfect choice. If ever a bird could sit in a tree and jeer at a frustrated cat, that would be the place. Indeed, I suspect that here we have an intimate partnership between plant and animal. The hawthorns produce masses of small red berries designed to be eaten by birds, who then carry away the seeds, and deposit them, well fertilized, in places where they have a chance to grow. (Bird guano, be it noted, is an ideal fertilizer for tree seedlings, rich in phosphoric compounds and fairly high in nitrates, both of which the seedlings need, but low in potassium, an overdose of which would interfere with their root growth.) The hawthorns probably developed their first small spikes to discourage browsing by deer, but the thicket of armament they have since developed is far beyond anything needed for self-defence. It serves a different purpose, providing a safe retreat, close to the ground, for small, seed-eating birds. Any predator would have to be truly desperate to try scampering up the trunk of a cockspur thorn.

Leah's first feeder was made of cardboard, and hung from the thorn tree by shop-string. She filled it with a scavenged mixture of seeds and breadcrumbs. When it actually attracted a few finches and blue jays, I relented, and helped her put up something more permanent.

Within a few days we had finches by the dozen, filling the tree with colour, and the air with twittering song. At least a hundred, if you counted both goldfinches and grosbeaks and two male purple finches, which Corky quite rightly calls rose finches, using the English name which describes them so much better than ours, for they are not purple at all, but a lovely soft rose-red. We appreciate them all the more because they are rare visitors to our dooryard, since the two thousand spruces and pines that Corky planted six years ago are not yet big enough to bear seeds for winter birds – though one of the white pines that I planted the year before has, indeed, produced a few cones, and even a six-inch seedling. Some years hence we will have bushels of wild birdseed in our trees, and a great variety of winter finches – crossbills and pine grosbeaks and siskins and redpolls, all of which are now but rare visitors.

To see flocks of crossbills you really need to climb up North or South Mountain into the few patches of mature evergreens that the pulp-cutters have not yet destroyed. Like the grosbeaks, the white-winged crossbills are bright and conspicuous at a time of year when the colours of nature are mostly subdued. First you will see one or two working to open cones in the top of an old tree. That is the reason for their crossed bills. They are specialized cone-openers. Looking more closely, you will see others that have been hidden by the thick foliage. Soon a dozen, or even two dozen, will appear, all industriously opening cones and stuffing their crops with seeds. The snow beneath the tree will be littered with scales from the dismembered cones.

The forest finches come to our place mostly in early spring. It is then we see the delicate pink redpolls, the flashing white-winged crossbills, the siskins, and the grosbeaks, as they pause near our house at the end of their migration, eating overwintered weed seeds and perhaps the few remaining cranberries from our marshes before heading up to the spruce ridges to build their nests.

The redpolls are among our favourites. They fly in close-knit flocks, bounding through the air, alighting to feed on overwintered berries. That is when you see how gorgeously arrayed they are, in soft pink and white, with brown stripes, and bright patches of red on their foreheads. Moreover, in this species the females, perhaps less vulnerable on their well-hidden nests than goldfinches or bobolinks, have colours almost as fine as their mates', with just a bit more white, a bit less pink in their feathers.

Goldfinches spend the whole year with us, the males putting on coats of brilliant black and yellow in the spring, darting and bounding above our meadow all summer long. The meadow is a bread-basket for finches, overgrown as it is with clover and knapweed thistle, field daisy and purple vetch, and a hundred other things that finches like to eat. They nest in the shrubs around the edges of the meadow, and sing from the tips of the tallest grasses and sedges. What songs they have too! Trills and runs that might make you suspect an Irish piper hidden in the trees. I can't imagine why anyone would want to keep a canary in a cage when he can have a yard full of goldfinches flying free. The goldfinches do not seem to be as strictly territorial as most small songbirds; we often see flocks of four or five bright males flying peacefully together in our meadow in May and June, flashing like scraps of congealed sunlight.

The feeding-ground of the goldfinches is the nesting-ground of the bobolinks. They are the other spectacular bird of the meadow, often mingled with the goldfinches, the male bobolinks singing on the wing, a few yards above their nesting mates, who sit quietly in the weed clumps pretending there's nobody at home. The bobolinks seem to prefer feeding among our garden plants, attracted there by beetles and caterpillars.

Occasionally in summer another gorgeous finch will perch for a while in one of our trees – the rose-breasted grosbeak with his bib of rose-red, his snow-white beak, his back and wings boldly patterned in black and white. He too is a fine singer, with a long, melodious, warbling song, richer and more musical than a robin's.

The seed-eating finches, as a group, are so gorgeously coloured, and sing so beautifully, that I think some explanation is needed. Why do these birds flock so closely together, flash such brilliant hues, and sing songs to rival the more famous thrushes and larks? Konrad Lorenz, pondering a similar question concerning the brilliant little fishes of the coral reefs, concluded that the colours were a kind of 'national flag' identifying each fish at a glance and preventing accidental trespassing on territories.

I suggest the finches wear coats of many colours because they associate in large flocks, winter and summer. The large flocks follow from their food supply: dozens of finches will feed in a single tree whose seeds are ripe. And because their feeding-territories are so compressed, their nesting-territories will also be close together, and in many cases shaded by the canopy of the forest. If peace is to be preserved in such conditions, a well-marked territory, no matter how small, is essential. Hence the bright feathers of the males. Perhaps, too, the songs, beginning to evolve as mere 'talk' between mates and chicks and feeding flocks, went through a phase of being national anthems, before going on to become the soaring aesthetic performances that they are today.

When you have greenhouses like ours that birds can fly into, the birds sometimes become trapped and confused, not knowing how to fly out again. When you have cats like ours you must be quick to rescue such birds. So I'm adept at catching small birds by hand, without hurting them, and without frightening them more than necessary. In this way I have caught a junco, a phoebe, a golden-crowned kinglet, a magnolia warbler, a yellow-bellied flycatcher, a redstart, a hummingbird, and a downy woodpecker.

Having caught a small bird, I always give it time to recover, holding it cupped in both hands, in the warmth and the comforting darkness. Birds are not claustrophobic. They react in just one way to a dark, covered place, warmed by body heat: they are back for a few minutes under their mothers' feathers, being brooded in the nest. They recover a sense of safety, a security they may not have known since their first free flight.

After a while I take the bird outside to the edge of our lawn where there are small trees with any kind of cover that they might desire. And then a strange thing happens. I open my hands, hold the bird out flat on my palm – and the bird does not fly away. It sits there in the sun, turns its head and stares at me for a long moment, as though puzzled by the vast mystery of life, then takes flight, heads into the trees, and does not return. But there has been a momentary flash of understanding across the gulf that separates bird and mammal, a renewal of the covenant that binds all living things together.

In fact, it is not uncommon for wild animals, when they find themselves *in extremis*, to seek out humans on the chance of receiving help. A dying herring gull once came close to our doorstep, and accepted and ate the food that we gave it. The food did not save its life; it died in the shelter of one of our hedges. But in other circumstances it might have survived with our help. The thing is that the wild creatures know such help is possible (if unlikely), and when they have nothing to lose they may try for it, as a last resort. I find a shade of comfort in the fact that humans, despite their unspeakable record of bloodiness, have extended help to other species in distress often enough for them to have learned, apparently at the instinctive level, that man sometimes holds in his hands the gift of healing as well as the gift of death.

The habits of birds are not as fixed as we might suppose – they evolve very rapidly to fit changed conditions. I remember a time when an evening grosbeak, in February, would have brought bird-watchers running from miles around. Now, every winter, there are thousands of them as far north as Newfoundland. They have learned to stay here in response to the human habit of putting out sunflower seeds for them to eat. As bird-feeders have become more popular, so evening grosbeaks have become more plentiful, until they have become *the* feeder bird of eastern Canada. If, for any reason, we could no longer buy birdseed in the supermarkets, there'd be a far-reaching disaster among evening grosbeaks – winter starvation of mass proportions – and the remnant would migrate, as their ancestors used to do, wandering southward in search of winter food, and coming back to nest in the northern summer.

18

The Forces That Shape the Earth

We are living in Glooscap country, on the shore where the figure in the Micmac creation myth brought Summer home from the south and banished the giant Winter to his icy caves in the far north. Could the Indian story-tellers have had a tradition of a time when the land was in the grip of perpetual winter? It's possible. Their ancestors lived through the last great ice age, not in Nova Scotia, perhaps, but somewhere along the glacial fronts of the mile-thick ice sheets that reached down from Labrador and the Northwest Territories as far as New York and Indiana and into parts of the state of Washington.

Glooscap explains very little. It is just a story, a creation myth, and no creation myth really tries to explain anything; it merely puts distance between ourselves and the mystery, helps us to forget how limited our knowledge actually is. As for the mystery itself, the ultimate beginning, no myth attempts to explain it.

Our own cosmology of the 'big bang' universe is a creation myth of this sort. Cosmologists will, perhaps, always be myth-makers, even when they are great scientists, for they deal with human minds and human limitations, with the kind of consciousness that can reach only so far beyond the limits of experience.

From what we can observe, from the data we collect by way of photo- and radio-telescopes, and by projecting such knowledge into the past, using mathematical models to assist our reasoning powers, we have come to believe that we are in an evolving cosmos, a cosmos whose history can be traced backwards some fifteen thousand million years or so to a single centre. At that point logic seems to suggest an explosive beginning, a universe emerging in microseconds out of a 'singularity,' a point or a cosmic egg or any kind of exceedingly dense beginning that we may wish to imagine. It is a beautiful, awe-inspiring myth for our own time, as Genesis was for our forefathers, but essentially it is just another means of creating distance between ourselves and the mystery. The mystery remains, as mysterious as ever. Instead of the primal chaos of Genesis, with darkness covering the face of the roaring deep a few thousand years ago, we now have a primal concentration of energy at a point fifteen thousand million years ago – which might seem to be a successful exercise in the art of distancing, until we remember that in the realm of thought no time is more than a moment.

Perhaps we can get beyond creation myths, beyond the feeling that we need a beginning, to a concept that unites time and eternity and includes the infinite. Fred Hoyle and his co-workers tried this with their models of the 'steady-state universe,' models that, unfortunately, failed to stand up to criticism or to account for the new data that came pouring in from the observatories. But I see no reason why infinity must deny evolution and temporal change or make them illusory, as the Hindu myths suggest.

The myth of the unfolding universe becomes even more beautiful for me when extended. The vision of our universe as a flower, opening by day and closing at evening, and opening again with the dawn, each flowering different from those that went before, with other flowers also blooming and fading, nothing ever wholly repeated, or having a true beginning or an ultimate end, is an inspiring vision wholly consistent with all we can observe or project within the limits of our present knowledge, and to me far more satisfying than looking back at a monstrous firecracker exploding some billions of years ago, its origins in nothing, its fragments racing toward oblivion.

The big-bang cosmology is a long way from Glooscap, as it should be; we have a far more complex culture than that of the Micmacs, and are capable of creating myths of far richer texture and more complex symbolism; our myths are adorned with pages of elegant mathematics, with subtle arguments to make them seem less like mere models, and more like divine revelations. But they belong to the same class nevertheless, stories that provide us with what seems to our minds to be a reasonable explanation of how things happened, all the way back to some point beyond which we cannot penetrate, beyond which looms the mystery, as large and unresolved as ever it was when pre-Columbian Indians sat around their fires hearing the soothsayers transmit the stories they had learned from the elders in their youth.

Back in 1605 a party of French settlers and fur traders, having examined and rejected other sites from the Saint John River to the northern coast of Maine, chose the Annapolis Basin as the ideal place to plant a colony. Three hundred and seventy-three years later a small family from Newfoundland chose to settle in the same place for the same reasons as the colonists: the beauty of the land, the fruitfulness of the soil, the gentleness of the climate, the variety of plant and animal life, the closeness of great forests and clear waters, the presence of the sea without its storms. But the full realization came to us only gradually: the understanding that we had come to live in one of the truly magical places of the earth. We care a great deal about this land, and about the changes it is undergoing.

For some three and a half centuries the land of Glooscap, the land of the Acadians, the land that has become ours, has been changing rather rapidly. The first settlers restricted the flow of the sea, drained the marshes, introduced new species of plants and animals, with little thought about the long-term effects of what they were doing. Today we are continuing such changes, and perhaps introducing others, even more far-reaching.

Any attempt to make use of the natural forces of the earth will change the environment to some extent. But change is not necessarily a degradation. A policy advocating 'hands off the environment' would be very short-sighted indeed. At the same time we should ensure that any developments with large environmental impact must be undertaken with the greatest of care and intelligence, not in ignorance.

The Churchill Falls power station was a great human achievement that altered the environment of central Labrador substantially – not, I believe, for the worse. Big power dams back up vast bodies of water. If you call this 'flooding' it sounds like destruction. If you call it 'making a new lake' it sounds like creation. In either case you are dancing the dance of Shiva, the dance of life in which creation and destruction are all part of the sustaining process. The major argument in favour of projects like Churchill Falls, the hydro-electric development at James Bay, or the proposed Fundy tidal-power project is that they produce enormous amounts of energy, nearly pollution-free, and go on producing it endlessly. They involve no burning of fossil fuels, no dangerous wastes, no acid rain, simply a modification of the environment, which may degrade it from the point of view of some species, but may equally well improve it from the point of view of humans and many other species.

At Annapolis Royal we have the first tidal-power station ever built in North America. It is a small plant, successfully producing electric power from a small tidal basin. There are problems: some fish have apparently been killed, including perhaps a few large sturgeon. There is some flooding of nearby farmland. But the problems are small, and easy to handle, compared with the insoluble problems of nuclear-power plants or the waste and environmental damage caused by plants burning fossil fuels. Tidal power, like hydro power, is clean. It will not poison the atmosphere or create radioactive wastes whose dangers will persist for millions of years. This plant points the way to a much larger development, along the same lines, a development that could put Nova Scotia a century ahead of the 'nuclear age.'

Every creature shapes and modifies its environment to some extent. Trees lower the temperature of a woodland by a few degrees in midsummer, and if there are enough of them, they help to create cloud cover. Gull colonies gradually convert rocky islands filled with shrubs and small trees into islands clothed by green turf. Humans do the same kind of thing macroscopically, tearing down mountains, draining portions of the sea, and driving superhighways across continents. This has led some people to say, 'Man shapes his environment, rather than being shaped by it' – a superficial judgment at best. I'm not a bit sure that humans modify their environment to any greater extent than earthworms, for example. As Darwin discovered, the changes a colony of earthworms can make in a patch of arable land are positively massive. An active colony of worms may deposit from ten to thirty tons of loam on the surface of each acre of ground, each year.

Humans do their work in more visible ways. Yet, all of their massive, world-wide undertakings added together come to far less than the environmental change created by the diatoms, those tiny photosynthesizers of the ocean surface who changed the atmosphere of the earth, making it poisonous to the anaerobic creatures that lived before them, but creating the very breath of life for the animals with oxygen metabolism who became the anaerobes' successors. There is a danger that human pollution could destroy the diatoms, and so indirectly cause more massive environmental change than human activity has done so far. There are a number of such dangers, but as yet none seems to be beyond the capacity of the natural world to absorb, survive, and to some extent correct.

The statement that man shapes his environment rather than being shaped by it sets up a false polarity. Shaping and being shaped are not conditions that exclude each other. The polluted cities are still shaping their inhabitants. They create strong environmental pressures for cast-iron lungs, bloodstreams that can handle high levels of poisons, and livers and kidneys that can metabolize and eliminate those poisons on a scale that human organs have rarely had to do before. Generations of city-bred humans have gradually lost their tolerance for sunlight. If exposed to the sun they may die of the highly lethal form of skin cancer called melanistic sarcoma. But their nervous systems have evolved a level of tolerance for noise that would probably have killed pre-industrial people. And so on. Examples could be multiplied. Eventually, if it doesn't come upon us with disastrous suddenness, we may even develop tolerance for levels of radiation that would have destroyed us all in the days before the Second World War. Some of the children born close to nuclear-power plants die because of radiation leaks. Those who survive have higher tolerance levels, and will transmit those levels to their descendants. But environmental pressure exists not only in such extreme instances. The rise in the so-called background level of radiation, if it remains below the critical point, will gradually breed more radiation-tolerant species of plants and animals, including humans. We adapt more slowly than fruit flies or mice because our generations pass more slowly; we might require two or three centuries to change as much as an insect can change in four or five years. But eventually the environment will shape us, physically, as surely as it shapes the mouse, the moth, or the microbe.

You cannot alter or improve even your back yard (as we have done) without destroying something. If you dig a lily pond you destroy the habitat of thousands of earthworms. If you turn a meadow into a lawn you destroy the homes of voles, shrews, garter snakes, toads, and numerous species of predatory insects that help to control pests. We have worked this widespread destruction on our own small part of the earth very nearly without a qualm. In every case we have created a new habitat for something else. Frogs live in our ponds. Herons feed on the tadpoles. The lawn provides for millions of earthworms, and flocks of migrating robins come to feed on *them*. If this is playing god, then that, indeed, is why we are here. It is the same with the megaprojects. Creating another great lake in central Labrador was neither 'good' nor 'bad.' A lake is neither 'better' nor 'worse' than a patch of forest. It is simply different, diminishing the habitat for deer but enlarging it for otters.

Had the Acadians debated the environmental impact beforehand, I do not think they would have changed their decision to build the dykes. And I doubt that the environmental debate will change our decision with respect to tidal power. I believe, though, that we will proceed with greater care because the debate is taking place, and that we will restrict the living space of other species such as birds and fish only to the extent we think necessary, and when we are convinced that they will find at least limited resources elsewhere.

The tidal flats are a great living nursery for plants and animals. The huge masses of seaweed, tens of tons of which we use for fertilizer on our garden each year, the billions upon billions of diatoms blooming across the flats, forming a visible green scum of microscopic plants, are major sunlight-converters, driving the engines of life on a scale that no banks of solar collectors so far envisaged could begin to match.

We watch it, we participate with it, in awe and wonder, but we do not shrink from the job of being human, either, of using the materials of the living world for our own needs, and the needs of others, animal and human, with whom we associate.

Most of the millions of species of animals that have become extinct were not extinguished by man. We have done our share, certainly, to exterminate creatures less than perfectly adapted to a world that includes such powerful creatures as ourselves, but we have done little compared to creeping ice sheets and drifting continents and sudden shifts of the earth's axis. The mastodons, the cave bears, the giant sloths, and the much earlier flying lizards, not to mention the vast marsupial fauna of the Americas, all passed into oblivion with no help from us. If, now, we are the instrument of death for the last remaining species of the great cats, the caribou herds, the elephants, and the great apes, that may indeed be shameful, but we should not look upon it as an unprecedented disaster to the world. We are doing what was done in earlier times by the growth of deserts, and the spread of the first large mammals. That is not, of course, an excuse for massive and unncessary attacks on the environment. But neither is it necessary for us to wring our hands and cry doom. We are part of the biosphere. We are changing it. For the first time in the history of life on earth it may be changed with caution, with foresight, with intelligence, instead of by the blind forces of chance.

19

The Tides Between the Stars

When the tides of Fundy fall into the far Atlantic, sucking the water of Annapolis Basin out through Digby Gap, a grim black island appears on the seaward side of our tidal flat. Looking out over the basin from our deck, beyond the tops of our peach trees, and between the big spruces on the shore, you can see this tidal island and its associated rocks any day of the year. And you can see seals resting on the rocks or in the shallows or on the island itself.

Seal Ledge, as the local people named it, sits like a plug in Fool's Run, between Porter's Point and Goat Island. It is a perfect place for seals, near the entrance to the two deep channels connecting the inner basin to the sea, with every fish that swims in these waters passing up and down the channels. At both ends of the island, and on either side of Fool's Run, are immense clam flats. No wonder the seals spend so much of their time just lazing in the sun. They certainly don't have to work very hard to feed themselves in the waters around Goat Island.

In September the population of Seal Ledge may rise to thirty or thirty-five. In February it may shrink to one or two. A few harbour seals come and go, but most of those in Annapolis Basin are gray seals – big animals that run to eight feet long and may weigh eight hundred pounds.

The gray seal is now so rare in Canada that it was for a long time thought to be extinct everywhere south of Greenland. It is one of the great scandals of Canadian policy that the gray seal is actively pursued and destroyed by killers hired by the federal government, and that fishermen also are urged, and encouraged by bounties, to pursue and destroy it. The excuse is that some commercial fishing corporations regard the gray seal as a nuisance; actually the slaughter is a make-work project for men I consider to be from the very dregs of humanity: killers who kill for pleasure as well as for profit. The gray seal massacre doesn't even have the excuse of the old harp seal 'fishery' that the pelts can be sold for profit. The gray seals have no commercial value. The carcasses are just left to rot on Nova Scotia beaches, or to sink, offshore.

I first watched the seals from our beach when we camped here in 1978, the year before we built the house, and discovered to my delight that they were grays, 'horseheads.' I had seen harp seals and harbour seals, arctic ringed seals, even giant bearded seals, but I had never seen a gray seal before. It was a special privilege to have this rare animal camping on my doorstep, even in a sense visiting my back yard when the tide was in, for the deed to our land includes the sea floor out to low-water mark (for all the good it may do us) and sometimes the seals will follow fish close to the beach. If one of them happens to be in a playful mood it will stretch out of the water and call to you in its mournful mooing bellow. If you row out to Goat Island in a rubber dinghy, one or two seals will sometimes follow you, for in the narrow waters of Annapolis Basin they are almost tame. They are used to people coming and going around their ledge; they are used to living here unmolested.

Strange that they should learn to trust humans so easily. The gray seal has no reason to be trusting. It is one of the most remorselessly persecuted of living animals. And yet, a neighbour of ours just down the shore at Deep Brook tells me that one of the seals comes to his wharf to be fed.

The seals that rest on Seal Ledge, turning from black to gray in the summer sun, as their fur dries and takes on the sheen of silver, are all far travellers. They have come here from their breeding colony on Sable Island, four hundred miles away, on the edge of the continental shelf. Even the pups have made the journey once, the adults probably many times. They go there every winter, raise their young to the age where they can swim, then disperse to their fishing grounds, a few finding their way to Annapolis Basin each year in March.

Adults and first-year young arrive here together and associate throughout the summer in what seem to be family groups. The biggest seal (doubtless the top-ranking male) takes the rock that first dries out as the tide falls. His favourite wife gets the next, close beside him. Younger males and females arrange themselves on other perches as these emerge above the water, until every seal has a place. Last of all, the silvery pups get the lowest levels of the ledge, which are often not completely uncovered, even at the bottom of the ebb. They lie there, bellies in the water, heads and back flippers arched upward, so that they look like new moons freshly fallen to the surface of the sea, afloat rather than aground.

But the members of this small herd do not always stand upon the order of their going. Sometimes one of the half-grown young will approach the resting place of a powerful adult. I have seen a pup swim up to the number two spot (occupied by the number one female) and stretch up from the water to nuzzle her and be nuzzled. I assume that this would be the seal's own pup, born six or seven months before. And the fact that you can see the grouping of father, mother, and half-grown pup together in August or September says two things about the social life of the gray seal: males and females remain 'mated' in summer when they are not breeding, and the bond between mother and pup lasts long past the time when the pup is weaned on the Sable Island beach.

The human explosion which began with the Industrial Revolution some two hundred years ago, and has continued with increasing velocity ever since, has altered profoundly the condition of life not just for humans, but for all terrestrial creatures. For the first time in the history of this planet the welfare of the biosphere lies in the hands of a single species. Whether you are an eagle, an elephant, a chanterelle, or a bandicoot your future, your very life, the survival of your race, depends upon decisions made by a species that has, at best, only a peripheral interest in your existence.

The extent to which we ignore non-human populations was shown when we began drilling for gas and oil in the ocean off Sable Island. No one even mentioned (then or later) that this is the last place in North America where the gray seal is allowed to breed unmolested. When the first accidental gas blowout occurred twenty-five miles from the island in February 1984, and poisonous liquids spewed into the sea for nearly five days before the well could be capped, no newspaper, no radio newscast, no television show even mentioned the fact that the gray seals were then on the Sable Island beaches with their new-born pups. I'm tempted to believe that no one connected with oil exploration, either in government or working for the drilling companies, even knew that the gray seals existed.

It would not be surprising if they didn't know. Everyone assumed for a long time that we had hunted the gray seal to extinction in Canadian and American waters. Its very existence was forgotten by all save a few marine biologists and a few seal-hunters in far-off Greenland. Most people have never heard that this creature was once present around our shores by the hundreds of thousands, much less that a few hundred breeding pairs are still alive.

The gray seal was the second large marine mammal to be hunted to extinction in the coastal waters of eastern Canada. The first was the walrus, which lived as far south as Nova Scotia in large breeding colonies when the first Europeans came here 'making trayne oil,' as Sir Richard Whitbourne expressed it. Trayne oil was lamp oil, rendered out of the fat of whales, seals, or walrus. The Magdalen Islands, Prince Edward

Island, and Sable Island were the principal (but by no means the only) resorts of the walrus in our region. By the time serious settlement began around 1600, most of the walrus had already been converted to trayne oil. More than five million of them had been butchered. By the late nineteenth century they were no longer found, except as strays, south of Baffin Island, and men had begun to think of them as an exclusively arctic species.

The gray seals, which also lived by the millions along our eastern shore from Labrador to Maine, were next in line for extermination. From 1600 to 1750 the gray seals were everywhere rounded up to be converted to oil for the lamps of Europe and America. Some two to three million of them, all told, went into the try pots. And then there were none. Some of the crews who exterminated the gray seals lived within sight of the little hill where we built our house three centuries later. Nicolas Denys reported in 1672: 'Monsieur d'Aunay sends men from Port Royal with longboats to make a fishery of them.' I can see Port Royal as well as Goat Island and Seal Ledge from my living-room window. But the 'fishery' could not have been pursued for long at Goat Island and Seal Ledge, where there was room for a breeding colony of only a few thousand seals, soon extinct. The great breeding herds were found in February on every island with a beach, but more especially on the islands south of St. Mary's Bay, one of which is still called 'Seal Island' though no seals have bred there in the past two centuries. By the dawn of the present century our grandparents had forgotten that the gray seal ever existed.

Until one day in the summer of 1949, when Dean Fisher, a field researcher for the federal Department of Fisheries, rediscovered them in the Gulf of St. Lawrence where they were believed to be long-since extinct. Surveys of the waters from the St. Lawrence estuary to Sable Island quickly revealed tiny breeding colonies at half a dozen places. Soon the 'Department of Fisheries and Oceans,' as they now grandiloquently styled themselves, launched a new – and continuing – war of extermination against the species, killing all the pups every year in every colony that they can reach with their helicopter gun ships, and as many breeding adults as they can catch. In official bafflegab this massacre, fully described by Farley Mowat in his 1984 book *Sea of Slaughter*, is called a 'cull.'

But even the Department of Fisheries and Oceans would hardly dare to send killers armed with rifles and machine guns into the narrow waters of Annapolis Basin, into the very back yards of a settled and peaceful residential area such as this. And so, a few gray seal survivors congregate every year on the ledges of Annapolis Basin, from Bear Island to the shallows near Port Royal, and up through Fool's Run to the clam flats off Ryerson Brook. Whether they will be permitted to remain, whether they will be allowed to reoccupy even a small part of their former territory, is for us to decide.

I find it difficult to discuss gray seals without a spate of anger that threatens to take over and dominate what I have to say. Writing about gray seals, or reading *Yucatan Before and After the Conquest*, I find myself drifting into a Mowat-like pessimism concerning human nature. Eiseley, having joined his 'star thrower' on the shore, tossing storm-wrecked starfish beyond the line of the surf, hoping that they might live, had the same kind of feeling: 'It was men as well as starfish that we sought to save.'

It is indeed difficult to believe that any creature as atrocious as the human animal can have an evolutionary future, that anything so opposed to the very thrust of life can be tolerated by the living universe. More comforting, perhaps, to speculate that we are going the way of the dinosaurs, making room for something entirely different, something as unimaginable to us as we would have been to triceratops.

Or there is always the possibility, more acceptable to me, as a human, that 'life,' 'intelligence,' 'spirit,' could be carried forward by those miraculous electronic creations that we still call machines, though they have just about as much in common with James Watt's steam engine as a videotape has with the

Rosetta stone. I see nothing inherently repellent in the idea of the human era being succeeded by the era of electronic intelligence.

Our thinking creations are still at a very primitive level – indeed, they are barely at the moment of their birth – but there is no reason to believe that they must remain so. We have given the gift of thought to such humble substances as silicon. Bits of glass and steel wire and the like have taken life out to the moons of the massive planets and beyond. We can, eventually, endow this life with capacities for self-criticism and self-improvement, for spiritual and aesthetic as well as intellectual adventure (indeed, I am not sure such qualities can be sepa-rated, but may be all part of the one cloth), and we can set it free to become the noösphere not just of the earth, but of all the bodies that circle the great lifespring of our sun.

There has been much speculation about whether life is possible on any planet in our system other than the earth. Perhaps animal life is not, but electronic life most certainly is. Even on the surface of Pluto, at the edge of the sun's domain, the cold rays from the heart of our living sphere could be transmuted into electronic thought, into glowing pictures, into sublime music; and the whole system could be wrapped in a web of electronic waves speaking to all its parts, and to other systems beyond it, forming a living whole incomparably grander than anything we have been able to imagine on this mere speck of a planet.

Such life, set free of flesh, would not only be able to live far beyond the narrow chemical range of animals and plants, but would also be freed of the atavism, the guilt, the horror and suffering that have made life on earth so tragic. I believe the tragedy is inherent in life as we have known it, that blood and agony, joy, and the upsurge of life and the shadow of death are all woven into the one cloth, indivisible; this is the very nature of animal life, the tragedy of life on earth, but I see no reason why it must be inherent in the nature of the universe. I can well imagine a new evolutionary leap, perhaps of the kind I have suggested, perhaps something quite different, that would redeem all the horror and suffering of the past. And when I think of such possibilities I think of 'god' not as a ruler handing down the 'laws of nature' from above, but as a well of inspiration springing up from below, flowing through such humble expressions of the living universe as gray seals and humans, but reaching out finally to clothe with life and thought and beauty every dancing atom of creation.

It is a long way off, yet, and may never happen, but we can certainly foresee the possibility of a conscious, self-reflective solar system, a linked organism, which may contain a biological element, or may not. The concept goes back at least to the time of Teilhard de Chardin's *The Phenomenon of Man*. Teilhard foresaw a fully integrated noösphere at what he called 'the omega point.' He also equated this with the ultimate human salvation and fulfilment. He did not suggest, perhaps never dreamed, that his 'human phylum' might vanish utterly before such an event occurred, and he limited his vision entirely to the earth. He was, after all, a Christian, believing in revealed truth and in the final 'redemption of all things in Christ.' He predicted a self-conscious planet with fully linked human consciousness as its brain or nervous system. That was all.

We can now go a good deal further. The earth may be no more than the fertilized cell, the zygote from which a living solar system, enormously greater and more varied than the earth could ever become, is to develop. Perhaps such a development is the normal course of evolution in any family of planets. Eiseley dropped such a hint in one of his later books, *The Invisible Pyramid*, when he remarked: 'To what far creature, whether of metal or flesh, we may be the bridge, no word informs us.' But he was speaking at the edge of night, out of a deep pessimism that bordered on despair. The vision that he saw was scarcely one of fulfilment, like the vision of Teilhard, or the one I here propose. Perhaps it is only since we have actually visited the Jovian moons – those regions of breath-taking beauty – and flown through the rings of Uranus that we are capable of putting these concepts, these fleeting visions, together into the vision of a living, intelligent solar system.

W. B. Yeats, in his reflective old age, remarked sadly that all life, measured in terms of his own life, seemed to be a preparation for something that never happened. Perhaps it is a preparation for something that has not happened yet.

All biological life, intricate and wonderful as it most certainly is, may only be the egg from which electronic life is hatched: that form of life which is not bound within the narrow limits of the carbon cycle or the tiny temperature range of liquid water, but which, fed only by available rations of starshine, can go forward to clothe with the mantle of consciousness not just those few millions of specks in the galaxy that happen to be earth-like, but all cosmic bodies, great and small, making of them, in some distant dawn, a true fulfilment of William Blake's cry, who saw the sunrise as a numberless company of immortals singing: 'Holy, holy, holy is the Lord of Hosts; heaven and earth are full of thy glory.'

I have heard the objections: 'Machines have no feelings. Machines have no souls. Machines are not creative.' Tut-tut. The steam engines that pumped out the mines of Cornwall before James Watt observed his first tea kettle were certainly not creative. I'm not sure we can say the same about the still primitive but quite wonderful Mariners who flew past Jupiter and Saturn and Uranus. The germ of creation, of feeling, of 'souls,' may already be present in those primitive creatures, just as it was present in us when we were single-celled animals in the slime of the ocean shallows. They do not yet have the gifts of self-replication and self-improvement, but both are well within the range of possibility.

Perhaps most humans will always be revolted by the idea of a new and higher level of life, with capabilities vastly greater than their own. Most of us would be equally revolted by the appearance of archangels clothed in flesh. We would tend to brand as 'evil' any creatures with superhuman powers, and wish for the means to destroy them. Perhaps electronic life has been allowed to survive only because man still does not believe in it, only because it seems to the mass of men insignificant, something that will forever be a mere extension of the human brain. So the mammals must have seemed unworthy of the notice of the dinosaurs. How could those little rat-like creatures, useful as scavengers, perhaps, but otherwise not worth noticing, ever be taken seriously by Tyrannosaurus when he was lord of creation?

Every species is but a leaf on the tree of life. It flourishes for a season, then withers and drops away, and in time a new species buds in its place. So the gray seals will in time pass away, though they struggle, now, for their survival. So humans, soon or late, will also pass, for the human species, too, is but a leaf, a mortal efflorescence that must wither. But some species give birth to their successors, prepare the way for a new manifestation different from anything that has gone before. Some species blossom into a dead end. Some open new paths into the unknown, prepare new ground for the steps of the living universe. And that is the greatest of all accomplishments. If it should be our destiny, before we pass, to be the instrument through which the solar system awakens, in a new phase of evolution even more marvellous than the emergence of life from the sea, there is nothing we could crave of greater glory.

About Mathematics

If you are are one of the vast majority of people who abandoned mathematics at the stage of elementary algebra, or elementary calculus, and then proceeded to forget even that, you have probably been told that this is an insuperable handicap to understanding the universe. It is not.

Mathematics is an accurate and unambiguous way of expressing logic. It means exactly what it says, not something else. So it is a concise way of channelling thought, and this is its whole, complete, and only function. This is why it seems to have almost magical powers of prediction, and so on. It sets the human mind free of verbiage, of confusion, of fuzzy thinking, of the clumsiness and ambiguity of spoken language.

Don't let anyone frighten you with mathematics. There is no magic about it. It is just shorthand, nothing whatever *more than that. Everything that can be expressed mathematically can be written out in words: in English or Russian or German or any other language with an adequate vocabulary (and much, though not all, of it can also be expressed graphically in diagrams). A mathematical statement or equation, written in the symbols of the English language, is just as accurate, just as 'rigorous,' as one written in Boolean algebra. It takes longer to write it down, that's all.*

Every time a science writer tries to bamboozle you with claims of a knowledge that you can never comprehend, just remember that mathematics is nothing more than simple logic, and its notation nothing more than an extremely compressed way of writing down a sentence, a way that makes blocks of logic easier to combine and manipulate. If someone tells you that the grand conceptions of contemporary physics 'can be expressed only in the language of mathematics,' tell him to go stuff it. He may be trying to make a mystery of his in-group skills, like a member of a medieval guild. More likely, though, he's mathematically illiterate, and is simply repeating what he's been told to say.

I'm not suggesting that we can do without mathematics, any more than we can do without digital computers. Both are indispensable tools for rapidly manipulating data, making sure that the steps involved are truly logical, and making predictions from the data. The work that a computer does with symbols in, say, ten minutes could be done with the English language and a pencil, but it might take all the time between the founding of the pyramids and the first Mars landing to do it.

Those who have tried to equate mathematics with Universal Truth or Ultimate Essence have strayed very far from reality, like the savage who fancies that the names of things contain their souls, or the ancient Greek sophist who thought that the notes of the musical scale expressed the laws of the universe.

If a physicist should tell you that relativity or quantum theory can be expressed 'only in the language of mathematics' you can be sure that he's not a first-class scientist, not one who, like Einstein or Bohr or Heisenberg, ponders the ultimate questions, but a minor actor anxious to turn his craft into priestcraft.

Does God
Play Dice?

The real issue, the real question, is not 'Does god play dice with the universe?' It is, 'Can god create freedom?'

According to Einstein, god could not create freedom. According to all nineteenth-century science, all science following Newton, he could not. According to the theologians, and many other philosophers, god could create freedom, and indeed does so. And according to at least some interpretations of contemporary physics, she does, in a certain sense, create freedom.

Just how far such anti-determinism extends (if it extends anywhere) remains to be explored. The question whether or not human freedom of choice is an illusion was by no means settled by quantum mechanics. In any case, whether choice is free or determined does not eliminate the question of responsibility.

It is at least possible that god in fact creates freedom not only at the root level of quantum events, where chance is in effect eliminated by the statistics of massive numbers, but throughout the macroscopic universe as well. A free universe, in some sense not determined by the act of creation, would be an infinitely more complex structure than the divine clockwork envisioned by Newton. It is so complex, indeed, that I cannot even imagine the most generalized structure of such a universe, and doubt that anyone else can imagine it, either. But that does not eliminate its possibility.

About 'Dimensions'

Many years ago, when I first read Albert Einstein's writing, I got used to seeing the world in four dimensions. I hope readers aren't put off by the habit. We sometimes think of the 'real,' physical world as three-dimensional, which indeed it is, in a certain abstract sense. An immobile person with only one eye, and no other sense organs, would see the world as two-dimensional, and think of the third dimension as some sort of mathematical quality, different from the other three. The world he saw would be an extreme form of abstraction from the world the rest of us inhabit. Our three-dimensional world is the same kind of abstraction. If you think about it at all, you'll immediately realize that no three-dimensional object has any true reality without duration. It must endure through at least a small lapse of time; otherwise it is just an abstraction, something that can exist in the human imagination, but cannot be seen, handled, or sensed in any other way.

But just as time introduces a fourth dimension into the physical world, so life, dynamism, in a certain sense introduces a fifth. In a way that cannot be visualized, but is easily conceived as an algebraic function, life is at 'right angles' to the four dimensions of the physical world. In the living world change and duration are no longer contradictory; they combine into a new kind of unity, a reality different from the simple duration of non-living things. An infant, a child, and an adult, for example, can be viewed as a single object only because they are viewed from a new 'angle,' an angle that does not exist in the non-living world of four-dimensional objects.

Among other things that possess this quality of changing and remaining the same are a star, a solar system, and a galaxy – all objects that go through long and changing 'life' cycles while retaining their individuality. The very fact that we refer habitually to the life cycle of a star, while we do not refer to the life cycle of a rock or a house, indicates that we recognize an important difference between the dynamic object and the non-dynamic one, the object that exists in essentially four dimensions, and the object that has the higher dimension that we sometimes call 'life.'

Like many important terms 'life' is undefinable, but has a clear meaning nevertheless. We may choose to expand its meaning to include all dynamic objects, or restrict it to dynamic objects with certain specific chemical properties; in any case, the thing that has a life cycle will possess the quality of remaining constant in some special way through changes that may transform it radically.

On the Second Law of Thermodynamics

Entropy is a word meaning 'energy transformation.' It has come to be applied especially to the degradation of energy that takes place in every system where energy is transferred or changed from one state to another. Every system, living or mechanical, transforms some of its energy into heat, and some of this heat is dissipated, so that it can never be recaptured and converted into other forms of energy.

The second law of thermodynamics states that you can never get out of any system as much usable energy as you put into it. In other words, every synthesis consumes more energy than its products can ever produce. Since some of the energy escapes as heat, and the heat dissipates forever, the whole universe, the sum of all the systems, must be heading toward a 'heat death,' running down, so to speak.

Entropy has bothered nearly every modern thinker, often profoundly. It involves a deep paradox which demonstrates how very, very far we are from 'solving the universe.' Since it requires energy of a high order to hold any system together and make it function (a star, a man, a microbe), and since all energy is being slowly degraded into heat, it seems to follow that the universe as a whole is heading for a 'heat death' of ultimate disorder, when no more usable energy will be available for any purpose whatever.

The paradox lies in the fact that we observe the universe becoming more orderly as it grows older, not less orderly, as the second law of thermodynamics would seem to require. Stars and galaxies are far better organized than gas clouds.

Life is better organized than the dust and gasses of the planets. In both chemical and biological evolution we observe the opposite of increasing disorder.

In the early moments of the universe there was only energy, then fundamental particles, and, for a long time after that, nothing more complex than hydrogen atoms and a little helium, the two simplest elements. Millions or billions of years later, after the hydrogen had condensed into stars, the stars began to 'cook' the heavier elements and distribute them through space in supernova explosions. So instead of simple chemicals with only a few particles in their atomic structure, we now had a great range of elements, some of them with hundreds of neutrons and protons in their cores, and clouds of electrons around them.

Still later the simple elements, light and heavy, began to evolve into complex molecular compounds until, at a late stage of chemical evolution, in the seas and atmospheres of planets, we had exceedingly complex polymers, compounds with hundreds or thousands or even millions of atoms combined into many-folded cables and knots of most intricate design. Then, when chemistry had achieved the stage that we call 'life,' it began building more and more complex structures: cells, organs, bodies, societies, governments, world orders, integrated solar systems. Instead of running down, in the universal decay called entropy, the universe seems to be growing toward some kind of grand awakening.

But even if you dismiss all this as illusion, and insist that in some sense the explosive ball of energy of the big bang was actually a higher level of organization than living solar systems and star clusters and galaxies, the fundamental paradox remains: if the universe is running down, then something must be winding it up. If the winding up 'happened,' 'back then,' rather than throughout the universal life span, the paradox is not less. Moving the process to some distant point in time does not help matters in the least. There are no one-way streets in nature. There can be no one-way streets. So we have something like what Darwin called an 'abominable mystery,' a mystery in which one of the basic laws of physics seems to be not just flouted, but reversed, by all that we can see and know and subject to the analysis of thought. It is no wonder that everyone from Einstein to Buckminster Fuller has tried his hand at solving this riddle, without succeeding.

The second law of thermodynamics simply has to be balanced by some equally fundamental process that we have not discovered. Even the most elegant unified field theory, combining all known 'forces' into a single universal process, the theory by means of which physicists dream of 'solving the universe,' if it is ever propounded, still will not remove this basic flaw in our attempts to understand the natural order. The descent into chaos required by the second law is simply not happening, indeed cannot happen, but we haven't a clue as to how or why. The theory of an oscillating universe might push the problem a little further away, but not far enough. In theory, heat should dissipate forever; there is no known process by which it could be sucked back into the renewed stage of a universal expansion.

Teilhard de Chardin thought he had solved the enigma with his 'curve of increasing complexification' proposed in his Phenomenon of Man as a balance to the 'curve of entropy,' but no one other than his most ardent admirers agree with him. And Teilhard was in any case an eschatologist, one who saw the universe as moving toward a single grand climax in which such 'phenomenal' matters as entropy would no longer be significant.

Some recent writers say, 'The second law applies only to closed systems. Living systems are not closed. Hence the second law does not apply to them.' This merely begs the question. Living systems are 'not closed' only because they draw energy from outside. But unless the outside energy is infinite, sooner or later they will exhaust it, at which time the second law will apply to them just as surely as it does to a clock that draws its energy from the hand that winds it up. The paradox, the enigma, is as strong as ever.

Fuller simply rejected the implications of entropy out of hand. It is opposed, he said, to the law of the conservation of energy. This clearly is not so. He also talked about light velocity and relativity as though such discoveries had somehow invalidated the second law – which they did not. Instead of admitting the mystery, or trying to resolve the paradox, he buried it under a mass of verbiage. He was right when he said that the second law applies only to the tangible 'small slice' of the universe that we see and know, the 'here and now.' We might say with him that it applies to the universe of Newton, but not to the universe of Einstein. All very well, but that doesn't dispose of the matter at all, for we do not know why it fails to apply in the larger context.

This is perhaps the greatest, the most awesome, of the remaining mysteries: the origin, the sustaining power, the immanence of the organizing force. Energy, degraded into heat, infinitely dispersed, is somehow collected and reorganized and turned into life and thought and organic evolution. But we haven't the barest outline of a theory to explain it.

To seek the ultimate nature of the universe is to seek the ultimate nature of god.

You may hope for deeper understanding, but any ambition for final comprehension will be defeated. Sooner or later we will have a theory in which the paradox of the second law is resolved, but in the course of resolving it we shall discover some other 'abominable mystery' that the most elegant theory we can devise will fail to explain.

Sex and Evolution

J. Bronowski in his Ascent of Man *repeats the opinion – indeed expounds it at length – that sex 'drives evolution forward.' This idea has been repeated over and over since the days of Darwin until it has become a cliché. It stems from the old idea, now discarded, that evolution moves mainly by the slow accretion of very small changes. Sex does, indeed, spread such small changes around, and may spread them throughout an entire breeding population, sometimes to its benefit, so we have the well-known 'benefits of cross-breeding' among husbandmen.*

But it is now universally accepted that evolution does not occur mainly by the slow accretion of very small changes. It occurs in sudden leaps, as the result of mutations. And sex is a major force for suppressing such mutations. It slows down the pace of evolution by tending to eliminate mutants, or to make their progeny more 'normal.' It is, in other words, a conservative force, tending to produce not change so much as conformity.

Among viruses, which have no sex, a single individual can have millions of descendants in a few generations. Consequently, viruses are able to evolve into new species almost overnight. New species of influenza, for example, appear every few years. How long since we saw the last new species of mammal popping up among our flocks and herds?

Sex mixes genes. Yes. But by mixing genes what you get is mixtures, not radical new types created by mutation. The more thorough the mixing, by means of cross-breeding, the less likely is any radical new type to survive. Sex may help to spread an improved characteristic, provided it is sufficiently strong and self-

assertive to survive the dilution of cross-breeding. There's no doubt it can help to strengthen a racial group by 'injecting new blood,' as husbandmen used to express it. But this is not evolution in the broad sense, only in the very narrow sense of improving the breed. Sex is an effort at self-preservation by the species, not an effort at self-destruction. It is such an important stabilizing influence that it evolved not once, but repeatedly, in the course of terrestrial evolution. By mixing the gene pool in a breeding stock it tends to preserve the genetic integrity of that stock, to preserve, to immortalize, the species. But preserving and immortalizing a species is not evolution. Indeed, it is only by the kind of change which replaces and destroys old species that evolution in the broad sense happens at all. So sex is not a driving force in evolution. It is a brake.

The wood engravings by G. Brender à Brandis, previously published in Wood, Ink & Paper *and* At Water's Edge, *are reproduced here by the kind permission of the artist and Porcupine's Quill, Incorporated.*

⟦DOUGLAS GIBSON BOOKS⟧

PUBLISHED BY McCLELLAND AND STEWART

Other Titles

THE PROGRESS OF LOVE *by* Alice Munro

"Probably the best collection of stories — the most confident and, at the same time, the most adventurous — ever written by a Canadian."

David Macfarlane, *Saturday Night*   *Fiction 6 × 9 320 pages, hardcover*

FOUR DAYS OF COURAGE The Untold Story of the Fall of Marcos by Bryan Johnson

"A book that places Johnson in the first rank of political writers from any nation."

Walter Stewart
Politics/Journalism 6 × 9 284 pages, map and photographs, hardcover

THE RADIANT WAY *by* Margaret Drabble

"Margaret Drabble's *The Radiant Way* does for Thatcher's England what *Middlemarch* did for Victorian England . . . Essential reading!"

Margaret Atwood   *Fiction 6 × 9 400 pages, hardcover*

NO KIDDING Inside the World of Teenage Girls by Myrna Kostash

Every parent should read this frank, informative look at life among Canadian teenage girls today.

Women/Journalism 6 × 9 320 pages, notes, hardcover

RITTER IN RESIDENCE A Collection of Comedy *by* Erika Ritter

Wonderful, witty essays on the life of the modern urban female, set down in rittering prose.

Humour 5½ × 8½ 176 pages, hardcover

THE HONORARY PATRON *A novel by* Jack Hodgins

The Governor General's Award winning author presents his first novel since 1979 — a triumphant mixture of comedy and wisdom.

Fiction 6 × 9 352 pages, hardcover

PADDLE TO THE AMAZON *The Ultimate 12,000-Mile Canoe Adventure* by Don Starkell, *edited by* Charles Wilkins

The astonishing, terrifying journal of a father and son's canoe voyage from Winnipeg to the mouth of the Amazon.

Travel/Adventure 6 × 9 320 pages, illustrations and maps, hardcover

THE INSIDERS *Government, Business, and the Lobbyists* by John Sawatsky

The author who got the Mounties to talk now reveals the intriguing secret world of Ottawa's lobbyists.

Politics/Business 6 × 9 320 pages, hardcover

THE LIFE OF A RIVER *by* Andy Russell

The affecting history of a river from the ice-age, through Blackfoot times, to its planned destruction in modern times.

History/Ecology 6 × 9 224 pages, hardcover